## Praise for *Zero Risk Real Estate*

"Chip's is one of the most comprehensive programs I have ever seen. His process has been thoroughly road tested and created millions of dollars of investing profits for Chip personally. He definitely walks the talk."

**—Sharon Lechter**
Founder and CEO of Pay Your Family First;
coauthor of *Think and Grow Rich: Three Feet from Gold*;
*Outwitting the Devil*; and *Rich Dad Poor Dad*

"With *Zero Risk Real Estate*, Chip Cummings once again displays his deep experience and simple, fact-filled writing style. In today's world of high stock market risk and low (almost no) returns on savings, Chip convincingly shows how tax liens and tax deeds can earn you high profits with little or no exposure to loss."

**—Gary W. Eldred, PhD**
Best-selling author of *Investing in Real Estate, Seventh Edition* and
*Trump University Real Estate 101: Building Wealth
with Real Estate Investments, Second Edition*

"Tax lien investing is an awesome way to make a fortune and a difference at the same time. Chip has laid out the road map for anyone to follow."

**—Tim Mai**
Wholesale and foreclosure real estate expert

"Chip's nailed it—there are many ways you can make money in real estate, but nothing is quite as easy as this! Never have I seen something so simple to produce long-term wealth—and all with a guaranteed interest rate from the government!"

**—Bill Bartmann**
Billionaire businessman and best-selling author of
*Bailout Riches! How Everyday Investors Can Make a
Fortune Buying Bad Loans for Pennies on the Dollar*

"Chip has 'Pushed It Up' and opened the doors for the average investor! I speak to leaders and executives all over the world, and *Zero Risk Real Estate* is the type of investment strategy that should take center stage for anyone trying to build long-term wealth. As a former fighter pilot, I know the importance of having all the details covered—and that's what this book does. Proud to have Chip as a wingman, and you should too."

**—Lt. Col. Rob "Waldo" Waldman**
Author of the national best seller *Never Fly Solo*

"Without a doubt, networking with the right people accelerates the growth of personal success and wealth. *Zero Risk Real Estate* outlines a solid plan for networking with the key people in the real estate industry and using the real estate tax system to create a long-term passive income with returns that are guaranteed by the United States government. Chip is a true expert in his field, and I feel very privileged to have him as a valued part of my network."

—**Ivan Misner, PhD**
*New York Times* best-selling author and founder of BNI®

"Once again Chip has nailed it with his latest book on real estate! I have referred many people to Chip on this topic and this new work again proves he's one of the best in the industry. Well done!"

—**Tony Rubleski**
Best-selling author and president of Mind Capture Group

# ZERO RISK REAL ESTATE

Creating Wealth through
Tax Liens and Tax Deeds

# ZERO RISK REAL ESTATE

## CHIP CUMMINGS

WILEY

John Wiley & Sons, Inc.

Cover image: ©Iuliya Sunagatova/iStockphoto
Cover design: Levia-Sposato

Published by John Wiley & Sons, Inc., Hoboken, New Jersey.
Published simultaneously in Canada.

Limit of Liability/Disclaimer of Warranty: While the publisher and author have used their best efforts in preparing this book, they make no representations or warranties with respect to the accuracy or completeness of the contents of this book and specifically disclaim any implied warranties of merchantability or fitness for a particular purpose. No warranty may be created or extended by sales representatives or written sales materials. The advice and strategies contained herein may not be suitable for your situation. You should consult with a professional where appropriate. Neither the publisher nor author shall be liable for any loss of profit or any other commercial damages, including but not limited to special, incidental, consequential, or other damages.

For general information on our other products and services or for technical support, please contact our Customer Care Department within the United States at (800) 762-2974, outside the United States at (317) 572-3993 or fax (317) 572-4002.

Wiley publishes in a variety of print and electronic formats and by print-on-demand. Some material included with standard print versions of this book may not be included in e-books or in print-on-demand. If this book refers to media such as a CD or DVD that is not included in the version you purchased, you may download this material at http://booksupport .wiley.com. For more information about Wiley products, visit www.wiley.com.

*Library of Congress Cataloging-in-Publication Data:*

Cummings, Chip.
Zero Risk Real Estate: Creating Wealth through Tax Liens and Tax Deeds/Chip Cummings.
Includes index.
ISBN: 978-1-118-35647-0 (pbk)
ISBN: 978-1-118-45936-2 (ebk)
ISBN: 978-1-118-45935-5 (ebk)
ISBN: 978-1-118-45938-6 (ebk)
   1. Real estate investment.   2. Tax liens.   3. Deeds. I. Title. HD1382.5
   332.63'24—dc23

                                                              2012022965

Printed in the United States of America

V10017614_021720

*To my three great kids—Katelyn, CJ, and Joe*
*With a future that bright—you better wear shades*

# CONTENTS

# FOREWORD

*Ninety percent of all millionaires become so through owning real estate.*
—Andrew Carnegie

*Buying real estate is not only the best way, the quickest way, the safest way, but the only way to become wealthy.*
—Marshall Field

How would you like an investment that is safe, is secured by real estate, is administered by the government, involves no brokers, is enforced by state law, and gives fixed returns? This may sound too good to be true given the roller coaster we have been on in both the real estate and equity markets over the past several years, but it's real.

Many people have lost their homes due to the real estate bubble bursting, and the daily news has been full of stories about foreclosures and short sales. Millions of real estate investors have also been hurt by the dramatic decrease in real estate values. In addition, there are billions of dollars of delinquent real estate taxes due on properties across the nation. However, as Napoleon Hill, author of the international best seller *Think and Grow Rich*, so aptly observed, "Every adversity, every failure, every heartache carries with it the seed of an equal or greater benefit."

The educated investor understands this and recognizes the opportunity that presents itself when a market declines. One of the little-advertised ways to invest in real estate is through investing in tax liens and tax deeds. Tax lien and tax deed investing is not a get-rich-quick investment scheme, but it has stood the test of time and is a great way to invest in real estate.

Tax liens can offer a very high, government-guaranteed yield on an investment that is considered a passive investment and that is backed by the underlying real estate. At the same time, you have the opportunity to end up with the bonus of actually owning the underlying property itself, for profits that could be well over 100 percent. No other investment can quite match the unique benefits of tax liens and tax deeds.

To be successful with any investment strategy, it is important to follow a proven system. And this is particularly true in tax lien and tax deed investing. It's not surprising, then, that there is a rapidly growing amount of information about investing in tax liens and tax deeds on the web, in late-night infomercials, in books, and in regional seminars. Before investing in one of these programs, I recommend you check out the instructor. Make sure instructors are qualified to teach the subject—and better yet, make sure they teach from their own personal investment experience.

In *Zero Risk Real Estate*, Chip Cummings provides a step-by-step process to create your own real estate investment plan using tax liens and tax deeds as vehicles to build a real estate portfolio that will provide for you and your family. His proven wealth strategies around tax lien and tax deed investing can help you create a viable and sustainable business in real estate.

Chip's is one of the most comprehensive programs I have ever seen. His process has been thoroughly road tested and has created millions of dollars of investing profits for Chip personally. He definitely walks the talk.

So, again I ask you: How would you like an investment that is safe, is secured by real estate, is administered by the government, involves no brokers, is enforced by state law, and gives fixed returns? If your answer is yes, then let Chip be your instructor and your mentor in building your real estate business.

To your success!

—**Sharon Lechter**
Founder and CEO of Pay Your Family First;
Coauthor of *Three Feet from Gold: Think and Grow Rich*;
*Outwitting the Devil*; and *Rich Dad Poor Dad*

# ACKNOWLEDGMENTS

It always amazes me how much work it takes to pull off a great project like this, and it sure wouldn't be possible without the help and support of a lot of incredible people behind the scenes.

First, I want to thank my wife Lisa for her support and patience, which is unwavering—even when I'm running in many different directions and she doesn't quite get everything I'm doing. Big kudos to my kids for putting up with me during some late hours in front of the computer and a sometimes crazy travel schedule. A special thanks to my dedicated staff at Northwind International Corporation and Chip Cummings Unlimited!—especially to my production manager, Sean Silva, for his creativity and putting in some extra hours.

Special thanks goes to my fearless acquisitions editor, Shannon Vargo (you rock!), and the rest of the John Wiley & Sons, Inc., team who made things happen, kept the project on track, and ensured a great finished product. Elana Schulman and Susan Moran deserve a special round of applause for making it fun and putting together such a great finished product. Thanks also go to my agent, Cynthia Zigmund, for her hard work and enthusiasm. Separately, my chief editor, Dennis Ross, deserves a great deal of praise for spending a lot of extra hours and long nights poring over the text to make me look good and getting the whole thing to make sense.

In addition, there were some key individuals that I have had the pleasure of working with who donated their time, talent, and experiences with stories and practical tips to help readers understand key points. My sincere thanks go out to Jeff Richman of US Financial Funding, Josh Moore of IRA-LLC 123, and Tony Rubleski of the Mind Capture Group. I can't forget my "protectors" at Essential Title, Katie and Carol—you two make it entertaining! A big thank-you also goes out to the many county auditors and tax commissioners who have shared their experience and wisdom over the years. Sharon Yaudas in Delaware County (we'll fix it!), Pam Watkins of the Virgin Islands tax office, and Virgil Jones in Georgia—I don't know how you keep it all together and still smile the whole time!

Also a huge thanks to Josh Leng, Dave, Susan, Tony, Mark, and the gang behind the radio show for your support. Special tip of the hat to Dave Farrow and Alex Carroll for their guidance and enthusiasm as well.

And last, but not least, thanks to all the ZRRE students, clients, and supporters. Your excitement, ideas, support, and success stories make it all worthwhile. It is truly humbling to realize that I have played a small part in your success, and that I have the opportunity to make a difference in the lives of so many people out there! Thank you all.

# INTRODUCTION

**S**OLD! To bidder number 142!

I was just 18 years old when I first heard those words, and a feeling of sheer terror mixed with a naïve excitement ran through my body as I realized I had just purchased something. I wasn't sure what, but my friend Jim sat there and whispered "Congratulations—that was a good buy!" I certainly hoped so, since he was the one who had just nudged my hand up with the bidding paddle attached.

It's been more than 30 years since that day when Jim and a couple of other fellow real estate agents coaxed me into accompanying them to a hotel ballroom near Detroit Metropolitan airport for something called a *tax sale*. I was brand new to the entire world of real estate, but eager to learn everything I could about how to build wealth through investing in property, and these guys had played the game successfully for a long time. Little did I realize how valuable this little field trip and their education would be to my future success.

I can still remember the experience like it was yesterday. Walking into the crowded room, I watched as the auctioneer rattled off parcel after parcel, slamming down the gavel after each one. I had grabbed a bidder number when I walked in, but certainly had no intention of using it until Jim egged me on.

BANG!

Wow—that was it. The gavel came down, and when the dust settled I had just bought something called a *tax lien* on a piece of land in Ypsilanti, Michigan. It was a vacant lot that I had never seen, didn't know how to get to, and didn't know what to do with, but it only cost me $500. Of course, at the age of 18 that was my life savings.

Okay, Jim—now what?

After jumping through a few hoops, nine months later I sold the lot to a builder for $8,500—an $8,000 profit! Well, not exactly.

There were some costs and fees involved, but my profit was still about $6,000. Not bad for a young kid right out of high school. I later learned that the builder was also ecstatic, because the lot was worth over $13,000. He quickly put a house on the lot and sold it at an even greater profit.

So what happened?

How was it that a vacant lot with a value of $13,000 could be sold for $500 without anyone putting up a fight? As you read *Zero Risk Real Estate*, you're going to find out.

Welcome to the amazing world of tax lien investing. If you are like most people, you are looking for a way to build wealth, and you want to find something that's predictable, secure, and yes—risk free.

While nothing in life is ever completely *zero risk*, this is as close as it gets. Real estate has created more millionaires than any other vehicle in the world. Taxes are attached to almost every piece of property, and they always get paid one way or another. Neither of those two facts is a surprise to you, I'm sure.

But after more than 30 years in the real estate and mortgage lending industries, I've used many different strategies to build wealth. I've worked with thousands of people from all walks of life, and I've learned that tax liens can provide a rock-solid road to wealth. Tax lien investing is a simple concept, and it doesn't matter how old or young you are, what your education level is, where you are located, or even how much money you have—this is a way to build wealth, with virtually zero risk.

But let me be completely clear to you: this book, *Zero Risk Real Estate*, is *not* a get-rich-quick plan. It's a get-rich-slow plan! While it is simple in concept, it takes some planning, research, and patience to make it happen.

Of course, many of you are still skeptical about returns of 10, 16, 25, or even 50 percent on your money, let alone guaranteed or zero risk. But give me a few hours of your time, read the book, and I'll prove to you it's possible.

Thanks to a collapse in the real estate market, combined with the power of the Internet, the rules and opportunities of profiting through tax liens have opened up wide to anyone with a computer and a few bucks to stash away. I wrote *Zero Risk Real Estate* for you. I want to share with you my 30 years of experience, and give you the same chance that was given to me by Jim so many years ago.

Now it's *your* chance to reap the benefits of a rough economy: the fallout from foreclosures, short sales, job losses, declining markets, sub-prime lending, and a host of other factors.

It's *your* chance to learn the ropes of how the tax system works and how you can make it work for you.

It's *your* chance to learn how to select the right properties, areas, circumstances, and deals.

Just as I was fortunate to have the hand of experience holding mine over 30 years ago, now I want to hold your hand and show you how to create wealth and a secure future for yourself and your family, and how to do it with zero risk.

*Fasten your seatbelt—it's going to be a fun ride!*

# Downloadable Letters, Forms, and Scripts

Throughout the book, you will see many of the forms, letters, and worksheets that I and other investors have used in pursuing tax lien and tax deed investment deals. You are welcome to use them for your business, and to make it easier, you can access all of these forms electronically in Microsoft Word, Excel, and PDF formats at www.ZeroRiskRealEstate.com/Bonus.

Once downloaded, you can modify, reword, or even add your logo and customize them a bit. Here is a list of some of the files that are available for electronic download.

**Letters:**
- County Tax Lien Information Request Letter
- County Tax Deed Information Request Letter
- County "OTC" Purchase Request Letter
- Letter to neighbors regarding sale

**Forms:**
- County Tax Sale Information Request Form
- Property Evaluation Form
- Tax Lien Tracking Form
- Tax Deed Tracking Form
- Property Inspection Checklist (for deeds and foreclosures)
- 13-step Checklist for Success

**Scripts:**
- County Tax Lien Info Request Phone Script
- County Tax Deed Info Request Script

**Excel Database:**
- County listings, complete with contact information, interest rates, tax sale dates, populations, and phone numbers for every county in the country.

# DEMONSTRATION VIDEOS

To help you on your *Road to Success* in tax lien and tax deed investing, we have provided several educational videos that show you step-by-step how to do many of the activities described in this book. There is no additional cost to you to access these videos, and you can find them online at: www.ZeroRiskRealEstate.com/Bonus. Here is a list of some of the videos you will find:

**How-to Videos:**

1. Sorting Demographic & Geographic Lists
2. Creating Automated County Letters
3. GIS Mapping of a Property
4. Conducting Tax Record Research
5. Performing Property Due Diligence Checks
6. Property Research Tricks
7. Environmental Hazard Research

## IMPORTANT DISCLOSURE NOTICE

This publication is designed to provide accurate and authoritative information with regard to the subject matter covered. It is sold with the understanding that the publisher, author, and individual contributors are not engaged in rendering professional services. If professional advice or other expert assistance is required, the services of a competent professional should be sought.

As with any type of printed material, information is subject to change. All reference items, websites, addresses, phone numbers, and program requirements were current as of date of publishing, but may change from time to time. For current updated information and releases, go to: www .ZeroRiskRealEstate.com/Bonus.

Bulk quantities of this publication are available at a reduced cost for educational, non-profit, corporate, or association distribution.

For your convenience, I have highlighted certain topics and points that are not to be overlooked. Here are the icons used throughout this book:

 Important Tip—This highlights an important item that you need to make a note of for future reference.

 Stop—This illustrates a critical step that could cost you money if you skip or ignore it.

 Download—This icon indicates that this particular form is available for electronic download at: www.ZeroRiskRealEstate.com/Bonus.

# UNDERSTANDING TAX
# LIENS AND DEEDS

*Nothing is certain but death and taxes.*

—Benjamin Franklin

**B**enjamin Franklin first uttered those words in 1789, and I'm not sure that much has changed since then. Of course, the concept of taxes goes back much further than that, as recorded history shows that taxes have been collected from people by governments, monarchs, and kingdoms for thousands of years.

But what happens when people don't pay their taxes? Some go to jail, some may lose their property, or centuries ago they may have even been hanged. Nothing that drastic takes place in today's society, but taxes are still an important part of life, and they are vital for governments to provide services to their citizens. And with estate and probate taxes in effect, they continue even after your death.

But what does that mean for you? More importantly, how can the tax system actually provide a road to wealth for you and your family? That's what *Zero Risk Real Estate* is all about. For more than 30 years, I have been actively participating and investing in real estate, both personally and with clients and students from all over the world. While there are many ways to make money in real estate, nothing comes close to the long-term growth, stability, dependability, and relative safety of tax lien investing.

Another benefit of tax lien investing is that it does not take a large amount of money to get started. You can buy tax liens with anywhere from a few hundred to a few thousand dollars if you like. Obviously the more you invest, the more you will get back, but unlike buying homes the traditional way, it does not cost hundreds of thousands of dollars to get into the game.

I will not only show you how it's done, I will prove it to you through specific real-life examples of deals that my students and I have done. I'll give you the forms, letters, checklists, and exact methods that I have used to get deals closed. And at the end of the book, I'll give you a website where you can actually go and watch instructional videos of me doing actual real estate investment deals.

But *you* have to make the commitment to do it, and along the road many people will throw obstacles in your path. You see, we all know that family, friends, and associates may mean well when they try to give you advice. Saying things they think are going to protect you, they may tell you that tax lien and deed investing is a scam, too good to be true, or even illegal—*none of which is true.*

I call them *Gremlins*—well-meaning people who think they know what they're talking about, but really just end by mucking up the works. There are a variety of reasons why these Gremlins are trying to spook you away from something that is financially lucrative and which produces a high rate of return for you. Their good intentions are obviously to try to protect you from yourself. They probably just don't understand the entire tax foreclosure process, or there is also the possibility that they may simply be afraid of what will happen if you succeed. It is unfortunately true that people like to see other people fail. Why? To feel better about themselves. You see, since they are doing nothing to improve their lives, they want to encourage everyone else to do nothing. This way they can justify their behavior. If they see you going out and working hard and taking action, then they feel guilty for not doing the same thing for themselves. It's much easier to sit back and say "that will never work" than it is to go out and try to make it work.

In order to succeed in your real estate investment business, the first lesson I want to share with you is to stay away from the Gremlins. They will try to prevent you from moving forward and becoming successful. The best way to handle the Gremlins is to ask them if they have ever personally tried tax lien or tax deed investing. Most likely they have not.

Making changes in your life is a positive thing. If you feel you are stuck in a hole, you need to dig yourself out by shifting your thought process from "what if I can't get out" to "what is the fastest and best way to get myself out." Making the decision to get out of the hole, developing a course of action, and setting a goal to try something new is just the beginning. If you want to truly succeed, then you have to be willing to do the things that others are unwilling to do, like investing in tax liens and deeds.

Change takes developing the right attitude and being able to withstand negative influences. Change is what it takes to become successful in your endeavors no matter what you choose to do in life. Make a commitment and follow through. You won't be sorry. Don't worry—your friends and family will come around soon enough begging you to tell them how you did it, and pleading with you to share it with them.

## REAL ESTATE AND THE PROPERTY TAX PROCESS

As I mentioned, real estate and property taxes have been around since the beginning of time, and kings, countries, and governments have been collecting taxes for many different reasons since the dawn of man. Taxes are very much a part of everyday life. In the United States, similar to other parts of the world, owners of real property are required to pay taxes to their local government. The local government in turn uses these taxes to provide its residents with critical public services such as schools, roads, hospitals, transportation, libraries, and fire and police protection. Without these taxes being collected, public services would eventually cease, and mass chaos would ensue.

In more than 3,200 county and local jurisdictions throughout the United States, there are billions of dollars in overdue and unpaid property taxes. In just one county alone in Indiana that I was reviewing the other day, there is more than $55 million worth of overdue property taxes that are delinquent right now.

There are dozens of reasons why people don't (or can't) pay their property taxes. Divorce, death, financial problems, job loss, estate or probate issues, emotional distress, or foreclosure, to name just a few. However, if a property owner fails to pay taxes for any reason, the property is then deemed *tax delinquent*, and the government must take the necessary steps to bring the property back into compliance with the law.

These unpaid taxes take away money from municipalities—money they desperately need to use for community services. To be fair, local governments do not blindside property owners with sudden and unexpected action in order to collect past due taxes. They offer every reasonable opportunity, in terms of both time and payment options, for owners to make good and pay their tax bill. Property owners certainly know what their tax amounts are, and they are given advance notice of payment due dates in order to plan ahead. In most cases, when a property owner has mortgaged the property, the lender also established an escrow account to collect amounts to pay future taxes to make sure that the money is there when needed.

However, if the tax payments don't get made, there comes a legally mandated point when the government is left with no recourse, other than to try to recoup the taxes in other ways so that its public services and other citizens are not negatively affected by the reduction in tax revenue. So what are these other ways by which the government can recover taxes left unpaid by a property owner? While there are differences in how different states and counties recover these taxes, about half the states use what is called a *tax lien* system, and the other half use a *tax deed* approach. Both options give local governments a legal interest in the tax delinquent property, and allow them to do whatever needs to be done to get the taxes on that property flowing back into the public coffers.

Obviously, this is an unfortunate scenario for the property owner as well as the local government. Both are now saddled with financial burdens they cannot meet on their own. The property owner has a property that has become unaffordable, and the government has a property it certainly does not want to own, although they have a legal obligation to collect the taxes they direly need.

So to minimize the stresses to both parties, they seek relief from an outside source, a third party who can bridge the gap between the property owner and the government. This is where you come in. You are seen as the knight in shining armor and the savior of county tax revenues.

By you investing in tax liens or tax deeds, you are enabling the county to collect the taxes so that they can provide their residents with city services that they need and expect. In return, you benefit by receiving a legally mandated high rate of return (interest) on your investment, which is secured by the property and the taxing authority of the government. Since the county controls the tax lien or tax deed sale process, your investment is safe, secure, and legal. This is the basis for *Zero Risk* investing.

## WHAT IS A TAX LIEN?

Investing in real estate is one of the most profitable markets available today. It allows you to make money multiple times from one simple investment and can help you increase your net worth, cash flow, and financial freedom by putting more of your hard-earned money in the bank. If you are working toward finding new ways to earn and invest, then looking at real estate is a good way to go. And if you are just starting out in this business and don't know where to begin, then tax liens are the perfect vehicle to get your feet wet and start to learn how to make money in real estate.

Whatever type of property you may invest in, whether it is residential, commercial, or industrial, there are several taxes that are attached to the property that can make you money. Taxes can make you money? Yes! But only when you take the place of the government and the taxes are then owed to you! Taxes are levied in a variety of places with the purchase of a property or home, and when they are not paid by the owners, they become tax liens. Tax rates are determined by the state and county where you live, based upon the price of housing in your neighborhood and assessment rates.

Tax liens begin when someone doesn't pay their taxes on a property that they own. If the taxes become overdue, the county has the right to sell the tax interest (or lien) to someone else. Usually, people who owe the government taxes will be given a certain amount of time to pay them. If they don't get paid after that time, the tax lien turns into a certificate that can be bought by an investor. Whoever purchases this document will then be given certain rights over the property, and those rights can change after a given amount of time has elapsed.

First, let's go over the meaning and differences of *tax liens* and *tax deeds*, and explain how you as the outside investor can benefit financially while you help local governments get back to providing much-needed services.

In the simplest of terms, a *tax lien* is an interest in the property that gives whoever owns that interest certain rights to the property—*but not ownership.*

When a tax lien is placed against a piece of real estate, it means that the owner cannot sell, mortgage, transfer, or refinance it until the lien is paid in full. They cannot do anything that will affect the title of the property. Anyone who does a title search on the property will see the lien and not want anything to do with the property until that lien is satisfied. Of course there are penalties and interest that have to be paid as well on the tax lien, and that's where your opportunity comes in.

When you invest in a tax lien certificate, you are basically waiting for the owners to pay off the back taxes they owe, including the interest and penalties. Now before you get nervous, let me assure you that you do not have to play collection agent and actually go out and collect the taxes. The government has a built-in system to take care of all of the dirty work for you.

The county tax assessor, or treasurer, will still collect the past due taxes on the property. But you've been kind enough (or smart enough) to purchase the lien from them at a tax sale, and now you own the county's interest (called the *tax certificate*). The municipality that ends up collecting the tax payment will wind up sending you a check—complete with interest. So essentially what is happening is you are paying the taxes on that property for the person who owes them. Now instead of that person owing the county, they owe you. It's as if you gave them a loan to pay off their taxes.

Now we all know what it's like to loan money to someone and try to collect it. You end up chasing after them for what seems like forever and in the end you end up feeling like the bad guy for demanding to get paid your own money back! Well, think of the county as your own personal collection company. They do all of the hard work and they don't mind being made to look like the bad guy. They will use every method allowed under the law to get your money back to you, *plus* all of the interest and penalties that you are now owed. Sounds great, right? I'm sure your next question is "But how long do I have to wait to get my money"?

The payoff must occur within the statutory *redemption period* that is specified in the law. The redemption period varies by state, and could be as short as a few months, or it could last for several years. Your return on your investment is predictable, however, because interest rates on tax lien certificates are fixed by the local statutes and laws of the state where you purchase them. So while you may be waiting a long time to get your return on your investment, the return is guaranteed by the government and the rate of interest is much higher than you can get from other types of investing.

Rates vary from state to state, but average rates of return can be anywhere from 10 to 24 percent and can go as high as 50 percent annually. States with longer redemption periods generally pay higher interest rates on the certificates, as an enticement for investors. You are certain to receive a nice rate of return because you are investing with the government, and their record for eventually collecting is pretty high. So what if the property owner still doesn't pay? So that you can get a better idea of what happens, let's take a look at a recent example.

I went to a tax lien auction, and after doing my research I found several liens that were on properties that I felt would be good investments—meaning the properties were very marketable and worth much more than the cost of the liens. I purchased a tax lien for $5,100. The lien was already 12 months overdue and I knew in this jurisdiction that if taxes were not paid within 24 months, then they would go to auction. This meant that the worst-case scenario I was looking at was waiting as long as twelve months to get a return on my investment.

The interest rate I was able to get on this lien was 23 percent. I was given the tax lien certificate by the county, and my company's name that I used to purchase the lien was put in public records as the owner of this tax lien. Now all I had to do was wait and see what happened.

I received a phone call from a title company about eight months later asking me for a payoff amount for my lien. Apparently the owners went into default and negotiated a short sale with their lender to sell the property. However, because I held the tax lien, the property could not be sold or transferred until I was paid off in full. I did some simple math and conferred with the county to come up with the amount I was owed. It broke down as follows:

| | |
|---|---|
| Cost of the lien | $5,100 |
| Eight months interest at 23 percent | $782 |
| Penalties for delinquent payment | $288 |
| Total amount owed to me | $6,170 |

So in just eight months my $5,100 investment made me more than $1,100 in profit!

Just to be perfectly clear, a tax certificate sale is not a sale of land, but rather is a sale of a lien against the subject property. Delinquent taxes are advertised in local newspapers prior to the tax certificate sale, the sale is open to the public, and participants purchase the certificates as investments. The tax certificate sale itself is conducted in a manner similar to an auction. The bidders are essentially extending a loan at a specific interest rate in order to pay the delinquent taxes for the property owners.

All you really need to know is a general understanding of the tax lien certificate investing laws in the state where you purchase them. Tax lien certificates can be purchased through auctions or over-the-counter (what is also known as OTC) by anyone, anywhere in the world.

When planned properly, your investment is safe and free of risk as opposed to investing in the stock market or other types of investment methods. Another nice feature is that tax liens are also not affected by the fluctuation of the retail real estate markets. There's always a built-in profit if you follow the process and do your homework.

Tax lien certificate information is also readily available when you know who to contact and what to ask for, and many lists are available directly online. The trick is knowing which ones to buy and when to buy them in order to make them zero risk.

The absolute worst thing that can happen when the owner does not pay the taxes is that they end up losing ownership of the property to the government. Of course, since you now own the tax lien interest instead of the government, you can now foreclose on a property that you purchased for pennies on the dollar *and actually own it outright, free and clear!*

Yes, you read that right. A tax lien is superior in title to any other lien on the property, and this includes mortgage loans. What that means is that the tax lien is in "first" position on title to get paid. If you foreclose on a tax lien, then all of the other liens on the property that are below you (first mortgage, second mortgage, utility lien, and so on) all get wiped out. You now own this property with absolutely no debt on it.

## WHAT IS A TAX DEED?

A tax deed, on the other hand, means that the county has already taken actions beyond the tax lien stage. The taxing authority filed the tax lien some time ago, and has already legally foreclosed upon and taken tax possession of the property, and is now ready to transfer ownership of the property to you. This also means that you are buying the property for a substantial discount with an already built-in equity. But remember, there's a reason why someone decided not to pay the taxes, and your job is to figure out why. Some of these properties may be easements, landlocked properties (meaning they have no access to common roads), alleyways, or other types of property that have little or no value.

The best tax deed investments are properties that are purchased for at least 30 to 50 percent below the fair market value of the property. This way, you receive the highest rate of return on the investment and help eliminate potential risk.

Like tax lien certificates, tax deeds are also offered through public auctions or over-the-counter. The rules and guidelines for bidding on tax deeds can usually be found on the county's website or by contacting them by phone or in person. So that you get an idea of how a tax deed works, here's a transaction I completed earlier this year.

I purchased a tax deed at a county auction for $15,000. This included all of the principal, interest, and penalties the county was owed on the property, plus slightly more since I had to outbid another investor. I had already researched this property and found that by using some simple comparative market analysis (meaning looking at what similar properties were selling for in this neighborhood), this property was worth anywhere from $90,000 to $100,000 if it was fixed up. Before going to the auction I did a drive-by of the property, looked in the windows, and did a thumbnail estimate of what I thought the worst-case cost scenario would be to clean it up and get it ready to sell. I came up with a safe number of $10,000. I purchased the property and was given a quitclaim deed by the county. (Some jurisdictions will issue a Certificate of Title or a Sheriff's Deed, and they are all basically the same thing.) I started my repairs on the property and hired a Realtor to market and sell it for me. She found a buyer willing to pay $95,000 for the property.

So here is how my costs broke down:

| | |
|---|---|
| Buying the tax deed | $15,000 |
| Repairs to the property | $8,800 |
| Commission to Realtors | $5,700 |
| Closing costs | $3,150 |
| Total expenses | $32,650 |
| Sales price | $95,000 |
| minus: | |
| Total expenses | $32,650 |
| Net profit | $62,350 |

As you can see, there can be a great deal of money made in these types of transactions, as long as you know what you are looking for, and if you conduct the proper research in advance. By the end of this book, you'll know exactly how to structure your own deal and cash in for a nice profit.

So to summarize, buying a tax lien certificate is buying the actual debt owed on the property. You now are owed the taxes and take the place of the county. You have the right to collect this money, and if you are not paid, then you have the right to foreclose on the property and take title.

Buying a tax deed means the county has already finished the collection process. They have foreclosed on the property and the county typically owns it free and clear. Now the county is the one selling the property and you can buy it from them. Yes, the county will sometimes make a profit selling it to you, but if you invest smartly, then you will still make a significant profit when you resell it as I did in the above example.

## UNDERSTANDING REDEMPTION PERIODS

Of course no one wants to take away someone's property, not the government and certainly not you. As I mentioned previously, owners are given every opportunity to pay their past due taxes and to avoid everything we've just talked about. They are permitted to make payment anytime prior to the tax lien being filed, after a tax certificate is sold, and sometimes even after a tax deed is sold. These are called *redemption periods*.

Once a certificate is sold, the owner can still redeem the property for a certain period of time by paying the back taxes, penalties, and interest to the treasurer or tax collector. These redemption periods can last up to several years in some states.

 During a redemption period you cannot enter, access, or use the property.

It is important to note that during the redemption period, the owner *still owns the property* and has all the rights and benefits of ownership. He or she can still occupy it, rent it out, or even sell it. Of course if they do sell it, then the taxes are paid at the time of sale, and you receive your check. This is because your tax lien on the property becomes a matter of public record, and any title company that performs a closing or transfer of title on the property will have to make sure you are paid off in full before the transaction can close.

As a tax lien certificate holder, your rights are quite limited. You cannot possess or use the property, trespass, or alter the use of the property. This is actually a good thing, since you're just looking for a solid guaranteed investment, not to become a landlord. Your interest in the property is simply a *paper* interest.

In a tax deed situation, it is entirely different in most cases. Once a tax deed has been issued, you now own the property and have to take steps to protect your interests (see Chapter 4). In a few states, however, including California and Texas, there is still a right of redemption even after the sale. It is important to know what the process and time periods are in each state *before* you invest. There is a complete listing of the current redemption policies for each state in this book's Appendix B. Since these policies change periodically, always check with the county or state tax office.

In some cases, you do actually have increased rights during these redemption periods. In Texas, for example, you are entitled to any rents, leases, or oil/mineral lease revenues during the redemption period, even if the property ends up being redeemed. What this means is that if the owner of the property has a tenant living in it, you can require that tenant to pay their rent directly to you and not to the owner. This means you will make money on your investment, not only when it gets paid off but each and every month you are waiting and the property is leased.

## What About the Real Estate Market Collapse?

It is certainly no secret that the real estate market has undergone and continues to go through some major corrections across the country. Okay, a collapse is probably a better term. So how does that affect your investment, or your decision on whether to participate in this type of investing?

Fortunately, investing in tax liens and deeds is not tied to the ups and downs of real estate cycles. Frankly, there are actually more opportunities to purchase tax liens and tax deeds in a down housing market, as more property owners face financial hardships and are unable to pay their property taxes and their mortgages. Here is another example of how you as the investor can benefit from owning a tax lien certificate in a depressed real estate market.

You bought a tax lien certificate on a property in Florida for $5,600 at 16 percent interest in a bid-down auction. The owner defaulted on the mortgage to the bank, and no payments have been made for the last year, which is why the taxes didn't get paid—there was no money in the escrow account. The property was purchased by the current owner only three years ago for $275,000, but now they are trying to sell it for just what they owe on the mortgage: $213,000. Unfortunately, it's been on the market for over a year and they haven't received a single offer since there are other foreclosures in their neighborhood.

Time goes by, and finally the lender forecloses on the property and gets title to the home. But the delinquent taxes don't go away; they continue to accrue. One day, the lender finally gets the property all fixed up, hires a real estate agent, and sells it for $175,000. However, before title can pass to the new owner, all the taxes have to be brought current. At the closing, the past due tax bill is paid to the county, complete with interest, penalties, and fees. Of course, unknown to them, you hold a tax lien certificate on the property, and a week after closing, you receive a check directly from the county, complete with interest on your money. Here's how your check breaks down:

| $5,600.00 | Tax certificate |
| $1,344.00 | 18 months interest |
| $6,944.00 | Your check! |

The property owner, the bank, or anyone with an interest in the property, had the right to redeem the tax lien interest at any time. Since redemption can also include not only the back taxes owed plus interest, but also fees, costs, advertising, maintenance, recording fees, and even sometimes your personal costs, it can get very expensive to redeem a property. If they hadn't redeemed, then you could have gone ahead and foreclosed on the property in the third year. Nice investment, secured with a $175,000 piece of property!

Now that you're starting to get an idea of how lucrative this can be, you may be asking "Why haven't I heard of this?" or "Why isn't everyone doing this?" Both good questions, and the answers are pretty simple. People just don't take the time to investigate something they are unfamiliar with, or they believe that when something sounds too good to be true, it probably is. This stops them from doing basic independent research, and realizing just how easy and lucrative these types of investments can be.

People are also afraid to take chances. Have you ever had an idea and said to yourself, "Man, if I marketed that I could make a million dollars"? Then what did you do? Probably nothing and went on working your normal job. Then all of a sudden you're sitting at home watching TV and there's someone selling *your* idea on an infomercial and you are sitting there screaming like a lunatic, "That was my idea!" So what made that person different from you? They saw an opportunity and acted on it. Most people don't, and that is why investing in tax liens can be so lucrative. Be the person who doesn't just read about it, but actually goes out and does it!

## WHAT MAKES THESE TYPES OF INVESTMENTS *ZERO RISK*?

There has to be some risk in this, right? As I previously pointed out, there is an inherent risk in anything, even crossing the street. The trick is to conduct your research and due diligence to minimize risks to the point where they are *virtually* zero. But when you compare them to other types of investments, the advantages quickly become clear.

Tax lien and tax deed investments are much better alternatives to investing in stocks, bonds, and mutual funds because they are more certain and more consistent. Second, there are no middlemen, and no commissions for stockbrokers or mutual funds, so all the profit is yours. You know your investment is safe because you are dealing with the government, and it's secured by their taxing authority. With a tax lien, you can determine exactly how much profit you are going to receive from the interest and penalties when the property owner redeems the property, and if the owner does not redeem it within the statutory period, then you can foreclose and acquire ownership at a deep discount. When you purchase a tax deed, you already know you are purchasing a property for pennies on the dollar with equity.

There is a saying in real estate investing that if you are doing it the right way: "You make money on a piece of property when you *buy* it, not when you sell it." Let me explain. When you purchase a stock, you have no idea what it's going to do in the future. You hope it's going to go up but you can't be sure. All you know is that the stock is worth what you paid for it today. But with real estate and especially tax liens, you can buy property with a built-in profit. If you buy a tax lien for $5,000 on a piece of property that is worth $100,000, you already know exactly how much money you can potentially make on this investment. You have locked in your profit when you bought it. You will simply collect your profit when you sell it.

But of course there are some drawbacks. Your investment funds will be tied up for a while. This is why we call this a *get-rich-slow plan*. Yes, there are other risks if you don't know what you're doing; we will address the majority of those in Chapter 6. We also hold regular Internet conference calls that are open to the public, so you can hear from professionals and experienced investors about how to avoid risks and get them down to practically zero.

Are you a gambler? I hope not when it comes to investment funds and your hard-earned money. Gambling contains risks. But think about a blackjack player in Las Vegas who holds a winning 21 hand. If you are that player, you know that your bet has zero risk, even if the dealer also has 21—it's a push. If the dealer busts or has a hand value under 21, you win and receive a high rate of return on your bet. Wouldn't it be nice to be able to see your cards in advance so you could know that you were going to be dealt a 21? Investing in tax liens and tax deeds means the deck is stacked in your favor. With odds like that, it's hard to think of any reasons why not to invest in them. *So, what are we waiting for? Let's dig in and get started!*

# GETTING STARTED

*The best time to plant a tree was 20 years ago. The next best time is now.*
—Chinese proverb

Since you now understand the incredible value and financial potential of tax liens and tax deeds, it's time to put that knowledge into play. But sometimes, the hardest part of any new adventure is just getting started. In this chapter, I'm going to walk you through step-by-step on how to find tax sale listings, how to research the properties, how to get some local help if and when it's necessary, and how to figure out how much to actually bid on the tax sale properties and certificates. First, though, we need to determine your investment objectives.

 There is only one of two possible goals you want to achieve when investing in tax sales—rate of return or ownership.

Each of these goals brings with it specific considerations that you must take into account when evaluating properties subject to a tax sale. If you are seeking a profit, then you'll want to focus on tax liens and the locations and bidding methods that might generate the greatest rate of return. If the interest rate is already relatively low, and the bidding method is a *bid-down interest method*, then you run the risk of ending up with an interest rate that could be as low as 1 percent or even zero. On the other hand, if the interest rate is high, you will want to balance that with the increase you'll face in competition with other investors, which tends to be the case in states with high interest rates.

If acquiring the actual real estate and building a portfolio of rental properties is your goal, then tax liens are not the most surefire investment vehicle for you. This is because over 95 percent of property owners (or a lender) will reclaim their properties within the designated redemption period. You'll make a nice profit, but you won't acquire a deed to the property. And even in the event that the owner doesn't redeem the property, whether you eventually acquire the deed at that point or not depends on each state.

Some states actually require another bidding process before you have a right to the deed (what is referred to as an *upset auction*). This means that after all the time you've invested, another party can come in at the deed stage and leave with the winning bid and the property. While this is not the norm, there will certainly be other costs to finalize your acquisition of the property. But this is why the most effective path to obtaining real property is through the purchase of tax deeds. As I mentioned before, only about half the states offer tax deeds for sale. With most of them, once you bid on and purchase a tax deed, the property is yours and you don't need to take many additional steps. With a couple of states in this category, however, there are additional redemption time periods offered to the property owner even after you've acquired the deed. Once these periods lapse, then you acquire the property. One final note is to make sure you understand the type of deed you're getting. It could just be a quitclaim deed, which means the owner relinquishes interest but does not guarantee clear title. In that situation, you would need to initiate a legal action known as a *quiet title action* to allow the court to establish and certify that you have title against all others. We'll cover this more thoroughly in Chapter 5, "Taking Control of Your Property."

 Tax deeds offer greater profit potential, but there are fewer available compared to tax liens, and they require more research and due diligence on your part.

Other factors that you need to consider include the geographic location you are going to focus on, where exactly these properties are, and how you can find them. And then once you do find them, how do you know whether they're worth it to you or if they're the right kind of property for what you're trying to achieve? The truth is that you're going to have to do your homework, because to get into zero risk territory, it's critical that you exercise good judgment and make smart choices before you even get to the auction stage. The preliminary work you do and the more research and knowledge you have about each property you plan to bid on will determine your success.

You need to isolate your investment strategy to ensure that your financial goals are well aligned with the type of property you target and the laws of the state in which you choose to invest. Once you're all set with your goals, then you can begin seeking out the right property. The property hunting phase can be a little tricky, but it can also be a lot of fun. Here are some strategies that will help you break it down.

## SELECTING YOUR LOCATION

Now that you've decided whether to invest in tax liens or tax deeds (profit vs. property), you're ready to focus on location, location, location! If you ask any real estate agent around, they will tell you this is a key element in successful real estate investing. Location is so very important because it will affect the property's appreciation and desirability as well as how easy or how difficult it will be to sell the property if and when you're ready to do so. This philosophy is true in tax lien investing as well.

Selecting exactly where to invest is really a personal decision, so you should think about whether you want to purchase your tax lien or tax deed in an area close to where you live or go out of state. Whatever you do, don't just jump at the highest interest rate. It's tempting, but there are many other factors to consider.

 Don't just look for property in the state with the highest interest rate—there are many other factors to consider!

If your purpose is to own property and purchase tax deeds, then you might want to start close to home so that it will be easier to manage the properties. Most states don't have any residency restrictions, so you can generally pick and choose where you want to invest based on criteria such as interest rates, redemption periods involved, the state's economy (those with the most foreclosures and job losses), or similar criteria. Maybe you will look at selecting an area where you would like to vacation or travel—the sky's the limit! Remember, in the tax lien investing arena, it is tempting to jump to the state with the highest interest rate for redemption, but you might have to attend personally to bid, the competition might be stiff, or the process of foreclosing (if the property doesn't get redeemed) might be expensive. With all that said, however, there are some really nice returns out there. Here is just a sampling of how you could break up your tax lien investment portfolio.

### Estimated Annual Returns on a Tax Lien Certificate:

Illinois: 36 percent per year. Liens with early redemption, 216 percent per year.

Indiana: 15 percent per year. Liens with early redemption, 120 percent per year.

Florida: 18 percent per year. Liens on early redemption, 60 percent per year.

Iowa: 24 percent per year.

Arizona: 16 percent per year.

My students, clients, and I have had really good success in these states, but again it's up to you to decide where you want to invest. Keep in mind that states that often have more competitive bidding at sales sometimes use the bid-down interest method. We will discuss the different types of auctions in Chapter 3, but with the bidding down ownership method, the winning bidder is the one who is willing to accept the least percentage ownership in the property. It's not a frequently used method, and certainly not preferred by us as investors.

A bid-down auction is where the interest rate at the auction starts at the maximum amount allowed by law inside in the county. Let's use 25 percent as an example. The bidding will start at 25 percent for a particular tax lien and people at the auction will *bid down* from that rate. So you may bid 24 percent, the next person bids 23 percent, and so on, until the bidding ends with whoever is willing to take the lowest interest rate on that lien. The county will still collect the maximum allowed by law for the lien (25 percent), but they will keep the difference between that amount and the final amount of the bid from the auction. So if you win this tax lien with a bid of 15 percent, then the county will keep 10 percent of the interest and then pay you the difference.

The bidding down interest method requires bidders to compete for the lowest interest rate they are willing to accept. Bidders cannot bid a rate that is higher than the state-sanctioned rate, and the winning bidder is the one who is left standing with the lowest interest rate. The delinquent property owner must still pay the statutory rate, but the local government will keep the difference as a premium, as shown in the example above. This doesn't always turn investors away, however, because there may be an opportunity to pay off the subsequent taxes on the property and receive the maximum interest rate on those taxes. This shows you that selecting a location by interest rate itself can be a little deceiving.

Another factor to keep in mind when choosing a location is that tax sales are most often held on weekdays during normal business hours. This means that you need to be sure you have the time and means to travel to attend the sales. As a new investor, choosing locations close to home may make it more convenient and feasible for you to fully participate in this type of venture. While some states may allow you to mail in your bid, or even participate in the bidding process online, attending the tax sale in person gives you a greater chance of overall success in terms of bidding, reevaluating properties, making on-the-spot adjustments in your strategy, and gauging the competition. There is a lot you can learn from watching other investors and bidders at work.

Start by researching your own county! Get familiar with how it works, operates, sends out sale notices, and conducts its auctions.

Another strategy might be selecting different areas of the country based upon when they conduct their auctions. Tax sales in Michigan are held primarily in August and September. Indiana holds a lot of its sales in March, April, and September. Some jurisdictions hold their sales once a year, while others may conduct a sale once a month. You need to find a pattern that's comfortable for you and your budget.

When selecting specific areas within a state or county, it is also a good idea to check with some local real estate agents, the local Chamber of Commerce, or the Convention and Visitors Bureau to find out about trends in the immediate area. They can help you with information on employment and corporate relocation trends, housing and construction, population and demographics, or even crime and health statistics. Some of my favorite sites to check for statistics include:

http://www.uscitycounty.com/all-us-counties.htm
http://www.realtor.org/
http://quickfacts.census.gov/qfd/index.html

If you are looking to invest in multiple areas or in more than one state, consider starting in one area and honing your technique before expanding to other areas. Laws and procedures vary from state to state, and even from county to county within each state. There is a learning curve here, and one size does not necessarily fit all. It is also recommended that you speak with a local real estate attorney if you have any legal questions about the process itself. As you can see, there are multiple issues to weigh, and you should always consider all angles before deciding on a location. Jumping at the seemingly obvious benefits may not always work out the way you hoped. In fact, many of the investors I know are tempted to rush to vacation spot areas like Florida to do their investing when they first start out. While that sounds great, there may be some terrific opportunities in your own backyard that you may want to check out first.

So when you are first starting out, it normally is best to stay close to home. Pick a county within a 45- to 60-minute drive of where you live. Drive up and down every street of that area and farm it. Learn everything you can. See what Realtors have signs up and are actively engaged in that area. Talk to local store owners to get a feel for the neighborhood. What types of people live there? What does the average house sell for? Are there a lot of empty houses in the neighborhood right now?

Take photos of the area and make notes about what services are nearby. For example, is there a school or a park within walking distance? Learn your market inside and out. Become your own expert. You know the saying that grass is always greener on the other side, so your county may end up being the best place for you to operate in.

## FINDING TAX SALE LISTINGS

Once you've selected a location that interests you, it's time to find the actual tax sale notifications and listings and compile your property selections. Remember that most states allow property owners to redeem right down to the last day before the sale, so as a result, you may find that a piece of property you had your eye on was paid off just days before the tax sale. We can avoid this scenario by making sure that we select several properties to bid on, and that the final list we compile is updated as close to the sale date as possible. Counties that have online access are going to be your best friend for this. Following are the different methods of finding out about tax sales and getting property bid lists.

### County Website

Most counties in the country now have their own website, so start by looking there. To find the county site, you can check on the Zero Risk Resource Center (see the last page of this book for access), or go to good old Mr. Google (www.google.com). If you don't know the actual name of the county, type in the city, such as "County for Atlanta, Georgia." The search results will quickly tell you that the answer is Fulton County.

The department within the county that is responsible for collecting the property taxes is usually the Treasurer, Tax Commissioner, or some other equivalent. So the next step is to search for that office. For Fulton County, you would search "Fulton County Georgia Tax Commissioner" and quickly find their website at www.FultonCountyTaxes.org.

You will also notice that this website is completely separate from the main county website. This is common in larger counties that have online payment systems for taxes, since it allows them to keep real estate records separate from other departments like Parks and Recreation.

Within the Fulton County tax website, they have an entire section dedicated to property tax sales. Different pages explain when the sales take place, where to go, how to register, and even the legal process that you need to understand when bidding on these properties. Sometimes they will even post the upcoming sale list right on the site, but during a recent check they still had an old list from 2004 posted. That won't help us at all, except that you can view the format they use and understand how the listings are arranged. In the case of Fulton County, we'll have to do some additional research to get their updated list.

But for websites that do offer a list right there on the site, it is usually either in a PDF format for printing or an Excel spreadsheet for down-loading. I love xls downloads, as then I can rearrange the listings and add columns to include my own research right inside the same file. I have some videos in the Resource Center that will show you exactly how to do this.

If you cannot find the information listed on the county tax website, then try a couple of the other county pages. The main county website home page might offer you a link to a third-party provider site such as an online auction company. There might also be links or sale information listed in a different department, such as the office charged with maintaining the actual real estate records. These offices are usually referred to as the *Register of Deeds, County Recorder,* or *Assessor.* While the terms for these offices can vary from state to state, they are consistent within each state, so it will be easier to locate other county offices once you get the hang of it. Believe it or not, some counties compile this data in their Probate Department, which is the last place you would ever think to check!

 As a shortcut, you can also just search the exact term, such as "Fulton County Georgia Property Tax Sale" and find the specific page you need.

### Call or Visit the County Office

The county may be too small to maintain a website, or maybe they just don't post any listing or tax sale information. Calling their office instead might do the trick, although it can sometimes be frustrating to find the right person with the information. Keep at it though, as someone inside that county office knows exactly what you are talking about. Be nice and cordial, but firm and specific. You simply would like to know when the next tax sale is occurring, and how to obtain a list of the sale items.

If the office is close enough to you, you may want to pay them a quick visit. Meeting these people in person is extremely valuable, and I have gained some great contacts (and struck up some nice friendships) with peo-ple in these offices. Don't be intimidated by them, but don't you ever treat them with anything less than total respect. I have seen people go into an office with a huge ego and an intimidating attitude, and that will get you nowhere fast (not to mention that it's just plain rude).

Also, don't be intimidated when you walk into the county office. Even the most seasoned real estate investor was a newbie at investing when they first started their career. We all started out learning from the ground up. Don't be afraid to ask questions or think that if you ask an obvious question someone there is going to laugh at you. The people who work in the clerk's office for the county are getting paid to expedite these tax sales. It's their job to help you! The best way to learn about the process is to ask them questions, be polite, and take lots of notes. I have been doing this for over 30 years, and when I enter a market for the first time, I still need to find out how that market may work differently than others I've invested in. I still need to ask the clerk questions. Remember, this is going to be your livelihood now. This is your business. If you treat people as professionals, then they will do the same for you and treat you the same way.

Once you locate the right person inside the real estate tax department, they will be able to provide you with a list of delinquent properties available for sale, as well as the date and location of the next sale. Make a note of the name and direct access phone number of the people you speak with. That will save you a lot of time later on, even after the sale, in case you have questions or problems.

Keep in mind that some counties hold sales throughout the year, while others designate just a few dates for sales each year. Many counties in Georgia hold a sale on the first Tuesday of each month. Because dates or times may change, however, always be sure to confirm the auction details directly with the county just prior to the sale. Also make sure to find out what requirements the county has in order to be eligible to bid at the auction. The last thing you want to happen is to spend weeks doing all of this research, get to the auction with your spreadsheets all ready, and find out you can't bid because you didn't fill out a form beforehand.

## Check Local Newspapers

Among the local government's responsibilities when holding a property tax sale is the requirement that they must post and publish a notice of sale in the county where the property is located. This is usually done in a newspaper or publication that has wide circulation within the county. It may not be your regular daily newspaper, but instead a legal publication within the county, and it will be out there somewhere. If you're not sure what newspaper to look for, then simply call up the clerk at the court and ask them where the tax sale notices are publicly posted.

The county is generally required to post the notice of the auction at least once a week for three or four consecutive weeks prior to the date of the sale. Notices or even signs may be posted right at the property as well. The company that handles the majority of county auction sales in Michigan posts a sign on every single parcel that is to be sold. Of course, if the property is still occupied, or a neighbor is trying to keep the sale quiet, the sign might conveniently disappear. Or even better, if one of your competitors has their eye on that property, don't be surprised if they've staked it out to make sure no one else can easily find out about the sale. I have known investors who pay people to simply drive around the market they invest in and make sure certain signs or notices go missing. So if a property is listed online or in the paper and there is nothing physically on the property to support the sale, don't assume it was a misprint.

## Tax Listing Service Subscription

There are some companies that compile tax sale property and auction listings. While I am not a big fan of these for several reasons, it can certainly be convenient and give you a quick glance of listings in your location of interest. Many will e-mail or text you updates on a daily or weekly basis, and include property information links that can save you a bit of time, but you have to weigh the cost. As part of our Resource Center, we provide a list of upcoming sales, with links back to the info page or listing page.

If you do decide to go with a listing service, remember that the information is always evolving, so take care to select a service that is frequently updated and has a reputation for reliability. Also keep in mind that no one is going to do as detailed a search on these properties as you will yourself. Especially if you are just starting out, I feel it is essential that you do your own research to learn how to find good deals on your own. Once you have this mastered and are investing on a large scale in multiple counties, it's okay to delegate some of this legwork to others, but not before then.

## Auction Request Letters

This is my favorite approach. Not only is it foolproof, since the county is *required* to respond to you, but it also eliminates some of the competition who are looking for the easy lists. By making it slightly more difficult to obtain the list, many people will simply not bother researching the county or the auction, or they won't know anything about it.

This method works extremely well for small- to mid-sized counties, and many times they will simply put you on an internal distribution list. I have received lists from counties by e-mail where there were only 5 to 20 people on the e-mail distribution list. Since the auction list contained about 100 properties, that meant a possibility of at least five tax certificates available per person. I like those kinds of odds. Fewer people bidding means more potential profit from each deal.

When sending a letter request to a county, there will be three things in the envelope: the request letter, a Tax Sale Information Request Form, and a return envelope. In Figure 2.1 you can see the actual request letter that I send out.

You will notice that the letter also asks them to place me on their distribution list for upcoming tax sales, and I include an e-mail address. Don't worry about spam; they are not going to be sending out your e-mail address anywhere, but I would suggest that you use a separate dedicated e-mail address that is different from your personal one and was set up just for your tax investing business. Even if it is simply a Gmail or Yahoo! e-mail, this will make your life easier later on.

As the letter indicates, also make sure that you include your contact information, complete with address and phone number on the letter. They may not use your envelope, but may instead enter your information into their computer system, or pass it along directly to their auction company. Either way, you want to be sure that they have multiple ways of reaching you. I have actually received phone calls from the county personnel, in the case of a rapidly approaching auction, or to make sure that I received the information I was looking for. Needless to say, those are priceless phone calls!

Next is the *Tax Sale Information Request Form* that I include with my letter. Figure 2.2 shows you the form, and you will notice that it is simple, straight to the point, but obtains a great deal of valuable information from the county.

The form not only asks about online versus onsite auctions, but times, dates, and listings. I've also learned over the years to ask about where the listings are published, what types of payments they accept, if there are payment plans (you never know unless you ask!), and what happens to unsold properties.

Getting their contact information is also key, and I ask about registration procedures, deposits, and even how many people typically show up. Can you see how this can put you light years ahead of the competition? Now you know why this is my favorite method.

You'll also notice that my contact information is right there on that form as well, just in case the items become separated. To finish it off, I want the name and phone number of the person who completed the form. This will quite often be different from the name of the person who is responsible for the auction.

## Figure 2.1
## County Tax Sale Request Letter

(date)

(title)
(county)
(address)
(city, state, zip)

To Whom It May Concern:

I am a serious real estate investor and am interested in purchasing one or more delinquent property liens at your next county tax sale.

So that I can be properly prepared for the sale, please provide me with the information on the enclosed form. I have also enclosed a self-addressed, stamped envelope for you to use for your response. If you have any type of e-mail notification system, please add my e-mail address below to your distribution list.

Thank you kindly for your assistance, and I look forward to a mutually rewarding relationship in purchasing these liens from your county!

Sincerely,

(name)
(address)
(city, state, zip)
(phone)
(e-mail)

Note: This form can be downloaded electronically at www.ZeroRiskRealEstate.com/Bonus.

## Figure 2.2
## Tax Sale Information Form

### Tax Sale Information Request

*Please provide me with the following information for your tax lien sales:*

County or Jurisdiction_____ State_____

When is your next tax auction scheduled? Date(s)_____ Time_____

Do you hold tax sales online? ☐ NO ☐ YES Website_____

If not, WHERE are your tax sales held? _____

Please list any and all venues used to advertise your auction. Please include scheduled advertising dates: _____
_____
_____

What form of payment do you accept/require at the auction? _____
_____

What are the procedures used for full payment of property liens purchased at your auctions? Do you offer a payment plan, or is payment required in full? _____
_____

What is your procedure for disposing of properties that are NOT sold at the auction? Do you offer them for sale afterwards? _____
_____

What is the name and phone number of the person in charge of disposing of these properties after the auction?
_____

How do I go about registering for your auction, and is an advance deposit required? _____
_____

When are your tax sales typically held and how often? _____

How many people do you typically get at a tax sale? _____

How many tax parcels are typically offered at a sale? _____

---

Thank you for your time and consideration! I have enclosed a self-addressed, stamped envelope for returning this form to me. If a parcel list is available for an upcoming auction, please include that with this form. If you have a mailing list or e-mail list, please include me on that distribution list. Thanks!

(YOUR NAME)
(YOUR ADDRESS)
(CITY, STATE, ZIP)
(YOUR E-MAIL)

Your Name_____ Phone_____

Note: This form can be downloaded electronically at www.ZeroRiskRealEstate.com/Bonus.

Finally, make sure to include a self-addressed, stamped envelope. While this may not be required, it certainly will increase the likelihood of your getting a response quickly. Once you start sending out these letters, responses will come flooding in within just a few days.

For those of you who want to send out multiple letters to several jurisdictions, you can automate the entire process using Microsoft Word and Excel. Using the *auto merge* function, you can have 100 custom-addressed letters ready to go in just minutes. To find out how, check out the free Zero Risk Resource Center, where we have a video that will show you exactly how it's done.

Again, be sure to get updates of the property listings in the weeks leading up to the tax sale. As owners pay off their taxes, properties will drop off the list on a daily basis, changing your strategies and research requirements.

 Get updates just prior to the auction! There is nothing worse than doing a bunch of research on a property that isn't available for auction any longer.

The more current you maintain your list, the more prepared you'll be with accurate property information and your bid preparation. It is a good idea to prepare an Excel spreadsheet so that you can keep track of the information as you go, or it could get overwhelming. You'll forget about properties you researched, or start mixing up the details in your mind.

Whether you are able to download a list or you create your own for tracking, you will at a minimum want to include the following information:

- Name of tax agency or county
- Parcel number (PID#)
- Owner's name
- Street address of the property
- City or township within the county
- Legal description of the property
- Sale date
- Minimum opening bid
- Tax assessed value

However you do it, keep it simple and organized. Lists can be coded in many different ways, and may contain information that is completely irrelevant for what you are doing. On the other hand, some listings will contain extremely valuable notes, including whether there are title problems, environmental problems, or a personal assessment of a recent visit to the property. I remember a recent auction where the property listing included a picture of the house along with a note that said "bulldozer bait." That saved some time!

Getting the list is the easy part. Remember, the government wants and needs to recoup taxes. They rely on these funds to provide municipal services to their residents, and they want to keep investors happy because they know how important you are to helping them recoup these funds. In order to facilitate that result, the law requires public notification.

So even if you run into some difficulty or lack of cooperation from county personnel, politely point out that the listings are a matter of public record. You may even get lucky and strike up a relationship with someone at the county who can help you with accessing the list.

Be aware, though, that larger counties may charge for a copy of the list. In areas like Los Angeles, Chicago, and New York, there are literally thousands of properties on the tax sale list. They publish a book as their list, and they can't do that for free. This works to your advantage, of course, since too many people will be too cheap and not spring for the few bucks to get a complete listing. That's their loss, as serious investors don't mind paying a few dollars for complete, accurate information provided directly from the county. The nice thing about these major cities, however, is that almost all of the information, once you have the listings, can be updated online. You'll know if a property was redeemed or removed for any reason and whether you should continue to research it.

Using the power of the Internet, and my letter-writing strategy combined with a little diligence and persistence, you should have no problem locating the list that contains just the right properties for you.

## FILTERING YOUR DATA

So you have a list—now what do you do with it? You need to sift through it quickly. Multiple lists with hundreds of properties, with thousands of pieces of information, can very quickly become overwhelming. So the first step is to cut through the clutter right away, and focus on the gems that are in there.

First, narrow your criteria and searches by:

- Property type
- Estimated market value or assessed value
- Sale date
- County

Don't get sidetracked, and keep your focus on deals that are within your geographic area. You might want to limit the number of properties you track if you are a new investor, in order to keep things manageable until you get the hang of the whole process.

Have an organized system for filing the lists, or use tracking software such as Excel. To make it simple, you may just want to concentrate on one list to start out. You will know when you are ready to expand your area or take on more information as you get the hang of it and get quicker at sifting through the data. To give you a better idea, I am able to cut down a list of 1,000 properties to 100 in less than 30 minutes.

Start by eliminating everything outside your target area, then cut out all the properties that do not fit your profile type or budget. Also eliminate the dogs in the list, such as teardowns, condemned homes, or inner-city properties. This way you avoid wasting time by focusing only on the necessary and relevant information for qualified properties. Let's take a look at how to evaluate the different property types.

## Evaluating Different Types of Properties

There are many different types of properties that come up for a tax auction, including residential, commercial, manufacturing, industrial, office, retail, vacant land, multi-family, condominiums, and special use properties—just to name a few.

 Get updates just prior to the auction. There is nothing worse than doing a bunch of research on a property that isn't available for auction any longer.

Unless you have specific knowledge in other types of properties, and until you gain valuable experience in this entire process from start to finish, then single family residences will yield the best results and returns since they are always in demand in the market. Also, more than likely, this is the type of property you have the most personal knowledge about. You probably live in one yourself. If you are looking at a property record and see the term 4BR/2.5BA, then you already know that means the property has four bedrooms and two-and-a-half baths. However, if you were looking at a piece of commercial property and saw terms like COO, ELR, and NPV, most likely you would quickly get overwhelmed trying to speak and understand this new language. So when starting out, stick to what you know, the single family home. But not all single family homes are created equal.

To stay organized, I created a simple *Property Evaluation Form* (see Figure 2.3). This allows me to track all the basic information in one place. It also makes it easy when it comes time to bid, since all my notes are right there.

## Residential

Within the world of residential real estate, there are three different categories—single family, multi-family, and 5+ unit multi-family. Any property that consists of five or more units is actually considered commercial real estate. Let's take a look at each type, as well as the two most common questions—mortgages and value.

**Single Family**    In general, single family residential properties are the most ideal for tax lien investing, particularly if they are owner-occupied. This is because there is always a demand for these properties, and homeowners typically have an emotional attachment to the property—meaning they will likely redeem.

 More than 95 percent of tax lien certificates on single family homes will get redeemed.

First, you should consider the assessment ratio of land to the improvements on the property. The ratio should be 30 percent or less to be considered valid, unless the land is waterfront property (which always has a high value and an easy turnover rate). For example:

| | |
|---|---|
| **Tax assessed value:** | $230,000 |
| **Maximum land value:** | $69,000 |

This means that the tax assessor has placed a minimum value of the improvements on the land of at least $161,000. To clarify it further, the land is worth $69,000 with nothing built on it, just as vacant land. The current structure sitting on the land is worth $161,000. So combined, the entire property (land and structure) are worth $230,000. You can find this information when researching the property files, which we will discuss in detail shortly. This ratio equation will eliminate excess risk in overvalued land, or properties that may be falling apart, or that are close to becoming bulldozer bait.

Second, an owner-occupied property is another big plus. A homeowner is invested in the property in ways that go beyond monetary considerations. They have built a life on that property, may be raising a family, and likely have other sentimental attachments to the home. What this means is that the

## Figure 2.3
## Tax Lien Evaluation Form

**PROPERTY EVALUATION FORM – TAX LIEN**

### PROPERTY INFORMATION

Property Address: _____

Parcel / Tax ID: _____

Legal Description: _____

Assessed Value: _____ Date of Last Assessment: _____

### LIEN INFORMATION

County/State of Lien: _____

Date & Time of Sale: _____

Location of Sale: _____

Purchase Price: _____ Mortgage Amt: _____ Interest Rate: _____

Original Loan Date: _____ Assumable? ☐ Yes ☐ No ☐ 1st ☐ 2nd

Property Type: ☐ Residential ☐ Vacant ☐ Commercial ☐ Other _____

Property Features / Assets: _____

AUCTION ID #: _____ Minimum Bid: _____ Fees: _____

Premium: _____ Costs: _____

Type of Bidding: _____ Other: _____ **MAX BID:** _____

### POST-BID INFORMATION

Receipt Number: _____ Date Filed: _____

County Contact: _____ County: _____

Address/Phone: _____

**Winning Bid Amount:** $ _____ PAID: $ _____

Total interest, other costs, and legal fees: $ _____

Total needed to redeem: $ _____

Mortgage Sale Date: _____ Redemption Period: _____

Investor Desire: ☐ Sell ☐ Keep Property: ☐ Listed ☐ Abandoned

Note: This form can be downloaded electronically at www.ZeroRiskRealEstate.com/Bonus.

likelihood of redemption is infinitely higher than on other types of properties. Bottom line: you'll get paid off faster and earn a nice return on your tax lien investment!

On the flip side, you should also be prepared for the possibility that, in the event of the owner's failure to redeem, you may need to recoup your investment by evicting the owner and foreclosing on the property. A few counties will handle the foreclosure process for you so you don't have to ever contact the owner, but this task is usually going to be left up to you. If there is a tenant at the property, you might want to contact the tenant and see if they want to stay on. This way you won't have to find a tenant and lose rent if you are planning on keeping the property and leasing it out. They are also the best prospects to sell the property to since they're already there.

I had a tax deed transaction recently where I did just that. I acquired a two-bedroom one-bath single family home for about $5,000, which the owner did not redeem. Since they didn't want to be evicted, I turned around and sold the home to the tenant for $32,000. The tenant was thrilled to buy it because the home was actually worth $75,000, and I was happy because I made a huge profit on the home, and turned it quickly without any marketing time, expense, or hassle—so it was a win-win for everyone! Better yet, I was able to offer it to them for almost nothing down, and I held the mortgage, which created a nice payment plan for them and an attractive income stream for me.

*Multi-family*   While they are harder to come across in tax sales, multi-family residential properties make an attractive investment for the same reasons we just covered, but you lower the cost per unit. If there is a single-family home that is worth $200,000 or a three-family that is worth $200,000, I will take the three-unit every time. Think about it: that works out to just over $66,600 per unit, and with the income potential, it is easier to sell to other investors at a profit.

The income potential from multi-family homes comes from the rents you will receive from the tenants, also known as the *rent roll*. Properties with high rent rolls are very attractive to real estate investors because they more than likely will provide the investor with a positive cash flow (also sometimes called a *cash cow*). This makes these properties easier to sell and will get you a higher return on your investment as well.

Of course, multi-family houses come with their own drawbacks. For one, you may be dealing with several tenants, which can get messy from an eviction standpoint. You also increase some of your fix-up costs if you need to foreclose, as you will have three sets of appliances, three water heaters, three furnaces, and so on. These types of properties will also tend to be a little more expensive when purchasing the tax certificate, and the competition will be stiffer.

Once you are comfortable with the overall tax sale process, and you have a few single-family deals under your belt, then it pays to start looking at these properties as the logical next step.

***Mortgaged Properties*** If your primary goal is to quickly make a profit from the interest rate on tax liens, then take a close look for mortgaged properties. With the number of foreclosures in recent years, and bank failures, mergers, and transfers of servicing of mortgages, there are a lot of properties that fall through the cracks.

If a property goes to tax sale with a mortgage attached, the lender must redeem it or risk losing their entire mortgage principal investment. I have been to several sales in which a lender representative has been forced to bid on a property and win at any cost. They were legally obligated to pay the taxes on behalf of the borrower, and they had to redeem or risk a lawsuit from the borrower. A real no-win for them.

On the other side, since no payments are being made during a foreclosure, then no money is going into the tax escrow account. Servicing transfers (this is when one lender sells a mortgage to another), or a simple decision based upon lack of funds, has forced the property into the tax sale. The bank will gladly pay the interest and penalties to redeem the property later once it is sold through foreclosure, since then they will have funds from the closing instead of having to cough it up from their other accounts.

Regardless of the reason, you are in a high lien priority position with the same rights that the county had. Tax rights always trump mortgage rights. That doesn't mean that the actual mortgage goes away; it just becomes a junior lien.

For you, this means that since lenders are naturally reluctant to abandon properties that serve as security for their loans, it is extremely rare that a mortgaged property will not get redeemed. So unless the property is a burden to the lender (i.e., the loan is much higher than the property value) where they've decided to write off the entire loan, the lender will redeem the property, resulting in a return for you. Remember, though, if you're interested in acquiring the actual property, be aware that lenders will often pay off the taxes right at the last minute in order to avoid having the deed sold. But if I have to choose between a lower guaranteed profit right now, or a potentially higher profit at some point in the future, I'll take the bird in the hand every time.

You will find a great number of these properties on the lists, but you need to research them carefully. As I mentioned, foreclosures and pre-foreclosures do not have payments coming in, and therefore no escrow or tax payments coming in. But that also means the property may have been stripped or vandalized. Unless the property is located in a really nice sub-division with high-level stable values and new homes, I'd make sure to get a firsthand look at it.

Obviously, if you are in the vicinity of the properties, then you will want to take the time to drive over yourself and take a look. Feel free to walk around the property, but be careful—don't go up to it or inside, as that would be trespassing. But if you can tell it's vacant, then don't be afraid to go to the property, get out of your car, and walk around it if possible. Take notes of all of the obvious damage you see if you can take a peek inside. You mostly want to know from the inside if all of the kitchen appliances are still there or if they were removed when the owners were forced to leave, as replacing these appliances could be a major expense if you were to take title to the property.

***Value > Taxes Owed***   It should seem like common sense that you need to seek out properties whose fair market value is far more than the amount of delinquent taxes. But how much more? A good rule of thumb is that the tax lien should represent no more than 3 to 5 percent of the assessed value of the property. On a tax deed, you can expect it to run 30 to 60 percent of the assessed value. Higher liens may indicate extreme past due water bills or other assessments on the property. I once purchased a tax deed which included a $12,000 past due water bill. The water pipe had burst during the winter, after the previous tenant had moved out. The water ran for weeks before someone noticed it running out the side of the house and called the city. Fortunately, with a tax deed, the water bill was automatically cancelled.

If you are able to identify properties within this sale range, it will mean that the owner will likely redeem such a valuable property or that you will be able to more easily turn a profit by selling the property if it comes to that.

### Commercial and Industrial

The higher numbers may make these properties seem more attractive, but as I stated earlier, these are not for beginners. These types of properties are very lucrative, but tend to require too much of an investment of money, time, and expertise for a new investor and are typically bid on by more seasoned professionals or investment groups.

The best type of commercial property to invest in is larger multi-family properties. Anything that is five units or more is classified as commercial, which would include apartment buildings, garden apartments, or mixed-use buildings that include apartments above a storefront.

There is also the risk that certain commercial or industrial use proper-ties will require a good deal of cleanup, environmental testing, or other investment costs beyond just the bid price. The taxing authority will let you know whether industrial properties may be subject to the Environmental Clean Up Act, the Spill Compensation and Control Act, or the Water Pollution Control Act, but this is usually done on the notice of sale and the bidder information sheet. That's rather late in the game to learn such critical information, so be sure to do your own homework beforehand. That being said, if you have an appetite for such properties, there can be a great deal of reward as well. I have participated in auctions that included a wide variety of such properties, including a cement factory, shopping mall, restaurant parking lot, flower shop, and a condominium clubhouse. I have even bought a lien on a lake parcel with a fountain in front of an office building.

I also recall a recent property tax deed sale that included an entire golf resort, complete with the course, clubhouse, and everything attached. The tax deed sold for just over $10 million. The value of the property? A cool $110 million. Not bad if you've got the cash to roll the big dice!

## Unimproved Vacant Land

This is the most common type of property available in a tax sale. When people run into financial problems, the first thing that doesn't get paid are taxes on some vacant parcel that's not bringing them any cash flow, and they can't sell. Usually it's because they don't know how! But vacant land can be a risky venture.

 Vacant land is the most common and the riskiest type of tax lien investment.

If there are no improvements on the land at all, you need to ask why. Is it too small to build? Is there a zoning problem? Or maybe it's an orphan parcel. And because the land is not improved, and hence is not owner-occupied, there is the possibility that the owner has not paid taxes on the property because he or she is not interested in it and simply abandoned the property. It could have been forgotten in an estate or been a part of a tug-of-war in a divorce.

Whatever the reason, this obviously lowers the chance of redemption, potentially leaving you with an undesirable property on your hands. But there are good deals out there on vacant land. If you decide to check out vacant parcels, you will need to first check ingress and egress to make sure that the property is not landlocked and that there is actually a road that gives access to the property, not just some undeveloped easement that will never be accessible. While many states actually do not allow landlocked properties, you could be in for a bit of a court battle to clear up the issue.

You also need to make sure basic utilities like water and electricity are either already on the property or can be brought to the property cheaply. The last thing you want to find out after taking title to a piece of vacant land is that the city water department doesn't service that parcel and now you have to spend thousands of dollars to have a well drilled.

On the other hand, buying a small strip of vacant land in front of a shopping center entrance could prove to be fun and interesting. Wait until the bargaining session begins, when you tell them that their customers can no longer enter the parking lot because you own the land that they have to cross! If there are minimal improvements on the land (such as an outbuilding), then as noted above, you should consider the assessment ratio of land to the value of the actual improvements. If the improvement itself is not an attractive draw, it may not be worth your time.

One very valuable way to invest in vacant land tax liens and deeds is on unimproved subdivision lots. If the utilities are in, and there are houses on the left and right of me—I'm in. I like these types of properties, as they are easy to sell to builders and developers who are looking to build a spec house in the development at a decent profit, and quickly.

Since these parcels can be picked up at a real bargain, you are in a perfect position to sell them on zero-down terms to a new buyer. This creates some incredible long-term cash flow with zero risk, since you'll recoup all your up-front expenses within the first few months. And if they default, you get to sell it again!

Wait a minute, what was that? You can sell it again? Yes! If you finance a property for a buyer and that buyer defaults, then you as the lender can foreclose on them. You take title to the property back, and now you can sell it again and possibly get another nice-sized deposit on the loan up front from your new buyer, plus another schedule of monthly payments.

I personally know of a bagel store owner on Long Island, New York, who sold the same store four times. Each time he would sell it, the new buyer would give him $25,000 up front and he would finance the rest for up to five years. The buyers would then default because the store wasn't making money, so he got to keep their $25,000 plus all the payments they made to him. He then sold it to a new buyer, received another $25,000 up front, and made the same deal. The moral of this story is, don't buy a bagel store if you have no idea how to run it!

## Special Use

There are certain types of what we call *special use* properties that can be very lucrative in your tax lien investing career. Since taxes are assessed on all types of property (except government buildings, churches, schools, or public lands), you will find tax sales that include highway or road right-of-ways, cell phone towers, lakes, parking lots, billboards, private easements, subdivision parks, and all types of oddball parcels.

At one recent auction, I purchased a lien on what turned out to be a cell phone tower. For a mere $200 I almost owned a multi-million-dollar tower right in the heart of the city. It eventually got redeemed, but no one else bothered to bid on it at the auction. Not a huge return, but it was fun and they had to pay all my expenses too! These special use properties are more of an advanced strategy, so I will cover this technique in more detail in Chapter 8.

## CONDUCTING INTERNET PROPERTY RESEARCH

Now that you've narrowed down your list, it's time to start researching everything about the property. At a bare minimum, here are the steps to take for a tax lien property:

- **Tax Records**—Go to the county treasurer (or commissioner) site, and enter the parcel identification number (PID). Most sites will provide information on current taxes, past tax bills, and when they were paid. Look for names and patterns to give you a clue as to what happened with the property. A name change over to an estate, for example, could indicate a pending probate case or family dispute.
- **Assessor Records**—Different from the tax records, these will indicate ownership history, land value, and any improvements on the property. Look for trends that are increasing or decreasing over the past few years. If it is a vacant lot, look for a change in the value of improvements; there could have been a fire that wiped out a previously beautiful home.

    Property lien records that show mortgages are often available online as well, many at no charge. Try to find out if there are any existing mortgage liens (or other encumbrances of record). Some states such as Georgia allow you to access all county recorded documents in one place for a low monthly fee (check out www.GSCCCA.org).
- **GIS Search**—GIS is short for Geographic Information System, and it is an online mapping system that shows the actual property lines as recorded relative to other parcels and improvements such as roads and easements. The systems have a graphical overlay on a satellite image that you can zoom in to clearly see all the details of the parcel. To find out if the county has a GIS system, Google search the county and

term, such as "St. Joseph County IN GIS". You'll get the hang of these maps very quickly, and you will get an enormous amount of information just by entering the PID.

- **Google Maps**—Google maps are an extremely valuable tool, but *never ever* rely on these maps to be an accurate representation of the actual property. I usually open two browser screens, and have my GIS system open in one, and Google maps in the other. Using a combination, track obvious physical property features from the GIS system in the Google maps page to make sure you locate the correct parcel. Pictures and images of property improvements can be very misleading, so trust the county site more than Google.

 Do not rely on Google maps alone to determine a property location; you may be several blocks away from the actual parcel.

For example, a recent search indicated a nice new home when I viewed the Google maps image. The street view was clear and inviting, but the aerial shot had too many trees to really see the home from above. A careful review of the county records showed that the property improvement value was $375,000 in 2010, and then it dropped to $0 in 2011. What happened? A fire resulted in a total loss to the structure and it never got rebuilt. The parcel was nevertheless extremely valuable, since someone thought enough to have built a $375,000 home there in the first place! The tax deed on that lot ended up selling for more than $22,000, which was still a real bargain.

Google maps are great (as are Yahoo! and Bing); just use them carefully to verify and clarify information from the county site. Here are the website addresses to use:

http://maps.google.com/
http://maps.yahoo.com/
http://www.bing.com/maps/

When looking at a tax deed sale, you need to go a little further to establish value and property history. In addition to the above steps, also do the following:

- Do a direct Google search using the property address. This will reveal any stories, pages, possible owners, and any MLS real estate listings that have existed on the property. Click on the search results and check out past list prices for an idea of rough value (although it obviously didn't sell for that), and other neighboring properties.

- Visit value sites such as Zillow, RealQuest, Redfin, eAppraisal, and others to give you a look at changing values for the property and area. This only works for improved residential properties, and the values can be off by quite a bit, but you'll get a good consensus.
- Check real estate sites such as Realtor.com or other auction sites for neighboring properties. Again, you are trying to get an overall feel for the values in the immediate area as well as the subject property.

Finally, if you have narrowed down your list and are serious about bidding on several properties, then you need to get a pair of eyes on it. Nice thing about that though, they don't have to be yours!

## RECRUITING LOCAL HELP

If it is not practical to personally visit the property, then you need some help. Fortunately, help is close by. A quick call to a local real estate office can put you in touch with a professional who knows the area firsthand. You can certainly ask them about the property or neighborhood, indicating that you have an interest in it, and that if you pursue it, you may be interested in speaking with them about using their services to market it later on. If you do this, however, be respectful of their time and effort and reward them if you do end up purchasing a few properties.

You can also find help on Craigslist. There are plenty of people who would be glad to take a couple of hours and drive by some homes to take pictures or even some video footage for you. Hire them for a few hours at $10 per hour, and tell them exactly what you want: 6 to 10 pictures of every angle of the property, or video footage as they walk around it. They can then e-mail you the picture and video files, and you send them a check or pay them via PayPal. This method has worked great for me, and I find students are the best recruits.

Another way to get some local help is by calling a lawn care company or snow removal service. Tell them you want an estimate on the property, and since you have never personally visited the property, you would like their estimate to include some quick pictures to match up with their bid. If you do end up getting the property, you'll have to hire them anyway. I once had a lawn service call me back informing me that the tenant there was cutting the lawn already. Funny thing, I didn't even realize I had a tenant there!

In Figures 2.4 and 2.5 I show an Interior and Exterior Property Checklist that will help to remind you of exactly what to look for when

# Figure 2.4
## Interior Property Evaluation Form

## *Interior Property Checklist*

Date of Inspection_____

## Property Address:_____

**Homeowner:**

**Contact Info:**

| Inside the Home | | |
|---|---|---|
| Smell: | Clean | Musty |
| | Air Freshener | |
| Cleanliness: | Good | Fair | Poor |
| Kitchen Impression: | Good | Fair | Poor |
| Floor Type: | | |
| Floor Condition: | Good | Fair | Poor |
| Cabinetry: | Good | Fair | Poor |
| Countertops: | Good | Fair | Poor |
| Appliances (if included): | Good | Fair | Poor |
| Sink Hardware: | Good | Fair | Poor |
| Lighting Fixtures: | Good | Fair | Poor |
| Ceiling Condition: | Good | Fair | Poor |
| Kitchen Notes: | | |

| | | |
|---|---|---|
| Bathroom Impression: | Good | Fair | Poor |
| Floor Type: | | |
| Floor Condition: | Good | Fair | Poor |
| Cabinetry: | Good | Fair | Poor |
| Sink Hardware: | Good | Fair | Poor |
| Tub/Shower Hardware: | Good | Fair | Poor |
| Lighting Fixtures: | Good | Fair | Poor |
| Ceiling Condition: | Good | Fair | Poor |
| Bathroom Notes: | | |

| Bedrooms | | |
|---|---|---|
| **Bedroom 1** | | |
| Condition: | Good | Fair | Poor |
| Size: | | |
| Closet Size: | | |
| Number of Windows: | | |
| Number of Outlets: | | |
| Floor Type: | | |
| Floor Condition: | Good | Fair | Poor |
| Bedroom 1 Notes: | | |

| **Bedroom 2** | | |
|---|---|---|
| Condition: | Good | Fair | Poor |

| | | |
|---|---|---|
| Size: | | |
| Closet Size: | | |
| Number of Windows: | | |
| Number of Outlets: | | |
| Floor Type: | | |
| Floor Condition: | Good | Fair | Poor |
| Bedroom 2 Notes: | | |

| **Bedroom 3** | | |
|---|---|---|
| Condition: | Good | Fair | Poor |
| Size: | | |
| Closet Size: | | |
| Number of Windows: | | |
| Number of Outlets: | | |
| Floor Type: | | |
| Floor Condition: | Good | Fair | Poor |
| Bedroom 3 Notes: | | |

| Important Things to Check | | |
|---|---|---|
| Inside: | | |
| Doors and Windows: | Good | Fair | Poor |
| Pipes (Plumbing): | Good | Fair | Poor |
| Mold or Water Damage: | Yes | No |
| Laundry Hookup: | Yes | No |
| Signs of Insects or Mice: | Yes | No |
| Smoke Detectors: | Yes | No |
| Standing Water: | Yes | No |
| Overall Floor Plan/Access: | Good | Fair | Poor |
| Crawl Space: | Good | Fair | Poor |
| Insulation: | Good | Fair | Poor |
| Furnace: | Good | Fair | Poor |
| Water Heater: | Good | Fair | Poor |
| Living Room/Family Room: | Good | Fair | Poor |
| Overall Impression of Home: | | |

Note: This form can be downloaded electronically at www.ZeroRiskRealEstate.com/Bonus.

## Figure 2.5
## Exterior Property Inspection Form

### *Exterior Property Checklist*

*Date of Inspection_____*

## Property Address:_____

| Pre-inspection Items: | |
|---|---|
| Homeowner: | |
| Contact Info: | |
| House Style: | Condo  Townhouse  Detached  Semi-Detached  Multi-Unit  Single Family  Co-Op  Other |
| Occupancy Type: | Owner  Rental  Vacant |
| Age of Home: | |
| Square Footage: | |
| Lot Size: | |
| Property Taxes: | |
| Heat Type: | Gas  Oil  Propane  Elect. |
| Air Conditioning: | Central  Window  None |
| Sanitary System: | Sewer  Septic tank |
| Water Source: | Well  Municipal |
| # Bed / # of Bath: | |
| Style / Stories: | |
| Finished Basement: | Yes  No |
| Parking: | Garage  Carport  On Street  None |
| Fireplace(s): | Gas  Wood  None |
| Pool: | In ground  Above Ground |
| Deck: | Yes  No |
| Fence: | Yes  No |
| Notes: | |

| The Neighborhood | |
|---|---|
| Neighborhood Style: | Brick  Frame  Mix |
| Are there many boardups? | Yes  No |
| Neighborhood Makeup: | Adult  Family |
| Neighborhood Listing 1: | |
| Address: | |
| Listing Price: | |
| Neighborhood Listing 2: | |
| Address: | |
| Listing Price: | |
| Neighborhood Listing 3: | |
| Address: | |
| Listing Price: | |
| Public Transportation: | Yes  No |
| Traffic Volume: | Busy  Moderate  Light |
| Condition of Street: | Good  Fair  Poor |
| Near Airport? | Yes  No |

| Near Train Tracks? | Yes  No |
|---|---|
| Near Factories? | Yes  No |
| First Impression: | Good  Fair  Poor |
| Positive Features: | |
| Negative Features: | |
| Other Notes: | |

| Curb Appeal | | |
|---|---|---|
| Type of Construction: | Brick  Vinyl  Wood  Pebbledash  Other | |
| Exterior Colors: | | |
| Exterior Paint Condition: | Good  Fair  Poor | |
| Driveway: | Yes  No | |
| Condition of Driveway: | Good  Fair  Poor | |
| Garage: | Yes  No | |
| Condition of Garage: | Good  Fair  Poor | |
| Condition of Yard: | Good  Fair  Poor | |
| Any Large Trees: | Yes  No | |
| Landscaping: | Yes  No | |
| Roof Condition: | Good  Fair  Poor | |
| Number of Windows: | | |
| Type of Windows: | | |
| Outside Lighting: | | |
| Direction Facing: | | |
| Front Door Condition: | Good  Fair  Poor | |
| Notes: | | |

Note:  This form can be downloaded electronically at www.ZeroRiskRealEstate.com/Bonus.

45

evaluating the property, especially for a tax deed sale. You won't be able to fill everything out, but it will give you a good start in helping to determine repairs, features, and of course your maximum bid.

Don't let distance keep you from getting a firsthand look at the property. Using these methods, you can purchase tax liens from Australia if you want to!

## 10 RULES FOR QUALIFYING EVERY PROPERTY

Once you get started researching properties, you'll quickly get the hang of it and get a system down that works for you. To help you out, here's a quick checklist of rules for qualifying each property that you consider. Follow these steps, and you will once again be looking at zero risk.

1. Once you receive the list of tax sale properties, immediately eliminate anything that is outside your budget, is located in the inner-city (rundown areas), or is outside your property type, meaning not residential.
2. Check the county's assessed value on the property. Eliminate it if the lien amount is too high.
3. Check assessed value history, and land vs. improvement value ratios.
4. Verify the PID, and check the treasurer's records for past tax payment history.
5. Check the Recorder's records to see if any mortgages or other encumbrances are present.
6. Visit the online GIS system to verify parcel location, boundaries, and features, including improvements.
7. Compare GIS imagery with Google maps to confirm research and visit the property virtually.
8. Check value sites like Zillow and Realtor.com for value histories and sales or marketing efforts.
9. Perform a Google search on the address itself to locate any other information about the property or neighboring parcels.
10. Set a maximum bid budget for each item, based upon your research.

## SETTING YOUR BIDS

The last step, after performing all your research, is deciding how much to bid for the tax certificate at auction. While much of this is more art than science, you should have a good idea of the value, property features, and history once you've completed the research steps above.

Bids on tax liens will go for less than tax deeds. This is because the potential profit is much greater with tax deeds, although the risk is greater as well. For a tax lien, remember that the bid should be in the 3 to 5 percent range of the value, although I have gone a bit higher than that depending on the quality of the property. You will have to use your judgment here, but don't get carried away.

For a tax deed property, I will go as high as 30 to 40 percent of the ultimate value, again depending on the type of property and how fast I think I can turn it. There are other expenses involved with the purchase of a tax deed, and those need to be factored in.

Once you set your bids, then make a commitment to stick to them! If you are getting outbid on every single tax sale item, then you know you will have to adjust your formula a bit. You do *not* want to win every single one! I attended an auction once where a gentleman kept bidding up almost every single property. He ended up with 17 houses, but the more experienced investors in the room knew he had overpaid and was going to take a loss on many of those properties. Don't be that person. I would rather you attend an auction and walk away with nothing than with a bunch of stuff that won't generate the profits you deserve.

Another thing to consider is not to get caught up in auction fever like the person I described above. You've probably seen auction fever in action when watching one of your favorite sitcoms on TV. The typical scenario is a person goes to an auction and for one reason or another gets caught up in the bidding process and ends up buying something they can't afford. I've seen the same thing happen at tax lien auctions.

The worst thing you as an investor can do is to fall in love with a particular piece of property. It is one of the classic traps newcomers to investing fall into. And it's easy to let happen. For example, if you've followed my program and done all of your homework on a piece of property, you probably have hours of your time invested in it. You've researched it online, maybe driven to it, inspected it, made a list of repairs or improvements you're going to make when you purchase it, and so on. You've spoken with people in the neighborhood about it. You've dreamt of the money you're going to make from this property. You are head over heels in love with this property and can't wait for the auction.

So what happens? Well, someone else at the auction has had their eyes on that property as well. They are bidding on it against you. You take this as a personal affront. "How dare they bid on my property!" So you get wrapped up in the emotion and keep bidding until you own it. As silly as this sounds,

I have seen it happen so many times. Now you have purchased a property and left yourself no room for profit. Remember, you make money on a property when you buy it—not when you sell it!

To avoid this takes just a little discipline. Have your spreadsheet with you at the auction and have on it a maximum that you can bid on each property to insure you will make money. Use the formulas I have shown you to determine what that number is. Then do not bid over that number. It may break your heart to see your property be sold to someone else, but remember—our goal is to make money.

Once you've accepted this fact and can stick to your maximum bids without emotion, you are ready to attend the auction.

# GOING, GOING, GONE!

*The point to remember is that what the government gives it must first take away.*

—John S. Coleman

Now comes the fun part—the auction! While you may certainly be a little nervous the first time you participate in the bidding process, you will quickly get the hang of it. Before we get there, you need to make sure you understand the different kinds of bidding processes that are used, and which one the county where you are bidding is going to be using for their auction.

In this chapter, we'll take a look at the different types of auctions and some strategies when you attend a live auction. We'll also check out a relatively new phenomenon for county tax sale auctions—the online auction. Of course, sites like eBay have been around for years, but now many counties are getting in on the fun and have opened up their auctions to investors around the world. But that doesn't mean you jump in with both feet without looking!

We'll talk about online auction strategies, what happens when you need to cancel a bid, and how to pay for your acquisitions. Another area that we'll cover is what is sometimes referred to as the *leftovers* or the over-the-counter market. There can be some real deals there as well. But to get a feel for how this whole concept of an auction came about, let's look at a little bit of amusing history.

## THE FIRST AUCTIONS

Records passed down through history from ancient Greek scribes document auctions occurring as far back as 500 B.C. At that time, women were auctioned off as wives, and in fact, it was considered illegal to allow a daughter to be sold outside the auction method. This same concept was used to auction off horses. Just like today, when you can preview the items at an auction beforehand, back then you could try out the horses and ride them before you decided to bid.

A *descending* method was used for these auctions, starting with a high price and going lower until the first person to actually bid won the auction, as long as the minimum price set by the seller was met. (Even 2,500 years ago the concept of an auction reserve price was enforced.) The buyer could get a return of money if he and his new spouse did not get along well, but unlike a horse, maidens could not be tried before auction.

Women with special beauty were subject to the most vigorous bidding and the prices paid were high. Owners of the less attractive women had to add dowries or other monetary offers in order to make the sale. Now, can you imagine having to be the auctioneer who has to tell a father his daughter is ugly and he needs to put up a dowry if he expects to sell her off at the auction? Makes you wonder just how dangerous the auctioneer's job was back then. Thank goodness times have changed.

## TYPES OF AUCTIONS

The concept of an auction is simple: get a lot of people together who are interested in obtaining the same thing, and let them bid against each other to get the highest and best price available for the seller.

For the buyer, the concept is equally as simple, but it comes from a completely different perspective: purchase an item at the lowest possible, deep-discounted wholesale price, or try to steal it.

Of course, most auctions end up somewhere in the middle for both winners and losers. Tax sale auctions are a little different though—there are no losers. Yes, you could say that previous property owners who fell delinquent on their taxes lose, but they are not on the selling or buying side at the auction. They lost a long time ago when they were unable to pay the property taxes, so the tax sale actually becomes a win-win situation for everyone else. The only way to lose at a tax sale auction is to do something stupid like not pay attention to what you are bidding on, get distracted, walk out without paying, or some other gross mistake.

It's a win for the county because they are able to recoup taxes that are rightly due for the citizens of that town. Remember, it's not the county's money, it belongs to the citizens and is necessary in order to provide for the operation of the county's services.

The buyers win because they are able to get a guaranteed high rate of return in exchange for providing the money to the county in advance on behalf of the property owner, and having that investment secured by the value of the property and the taxing power of the county itself to protect the investment.

The citizens of the county win, since they are able to insure that tax revenues are maintained in a fair and equitable manner to protect the operation of their city. And if there is an auction company involved, then of course they win by earning some commissions as well.

Auctions come in many different flavors. I have attended auctions where there have been several thousand people in attendance, and others that were held in a small room in the basement of a county building with just 10 people in the room. The good part about this type of auction is it's really easy to size up your competition.

As you might expect, auctions that take place in large jurisdictions tend to have more bidders in attendance, but that is balanced by the fact that there normally will be hundreds of parcels up for bid. In these large auctions, you'll find that some attendees are backed by institutional investment groups and have more to spend, making it a more competitive and challenging environment for you as an individual investor. In fact, some investment groups will have millions to spend. On the other hand, they will not be interested in the smaller and less expensive liens and properties, and this is where you'll find your niche.

Finding your niche is the key to succeeding at a tax lien auction. Don't start out buying every different type of property that comes up. Pick something you know and run with it until you have it mastered, then branch out into other areas. If you are looking to buy tax liens with the hope of eventually foreclosing on the property, taking possession, and then renting the property out, multi-family homes will be very attractive. Just make sure you pick a niche and stick with it and always know what you are bidding on. I have been to auctions where the bidding is over and the person who won the auction says, "So what type of property is that tax lien on, by the way?" Not a smart investment strategy.

Although these large auctions can be fun and exhilarating, to the extent that this level of competition at the auction concerns you, you should consider seeking properties in smaller jurisdictions with more manageable auctions. This becomes even more attractive when you consider that the interest rate and redemption periods are generally set by state law, so choosing a smaller jurisdiction within the state with fewer competitors will still garner you the same potential for return as would the larger, better-attended, more competitive auctions. An 18 percent return in Cook County, Illinois (Chicago), is the same as an 18 percent return in southern Pope County, where the entire population is less than 4,500 people.

However, that being said—*do not* let competition scare you. When you have done your research, and are ready to go, it should not matter where you are, what the jurisdiction is, or who the competition is. Your money is just as good as theirs is, and so long as you don't get carried away, then your purchase is just as sound. When I attend an auction for the first time, no one there knows who I am. The regulars will look at me as someone they don't have to take seriously, figuring I am there either as a new investor or just to watch and follow along. It's only when the bidding starts that they realize I am their competition and not the other way around!

As I mentioned, bidding procedures vary among states and counties. The most common types of bidding include premium, bid down ownership, bid down interest, lottery or rotational bidding, first come-first served, and random selection. Let's take a look at each of these.

## Premium Bidding

Most states and counties use what is by far the most common type of bidding, called the *premium bidding* method. This is the type of bidding you normally think of when you think of auctions you might see on TV. Essentially, the auctioneer announces the minimum bid for a property and the bidding starts there, and it then continues to rise as long as there are interested bidders. When there is only one bidder left, the lien is sold to that bidder for the price bid. The amount of the winning bid that is over and above the minimum is referred to as the *premium*.

If you acquire a lien through this bidding method, and the property owner redeems that property, you will still recoup what you paid, but a few states do not allow you to earn interest on the premium but only on the actual minimum bid. Again, make sure you check before going in. This is important to understand. If a tax lien owed by a property owner goes up for auction in one of these jurisdictions, then you can only earn interest on the delinquent amount of the tax and not on the entire amount you might have paid for the lien. So buying a $5,000 tax lien at this auction for $8,000 will give you ownership of the lien, but you can collect interest only on the original $5,000 that was owed. Keep this in mind when you're bidding and counting up your profits.

At a tax deed auction that uses the premium bidding method, the process is generally the same, but because you are bidding for a deed to the property as opposed to a lien, you generally need not be as concerned about the interest rate and whether it applies to the premium amount. However, in the few states that allow an additional redemption period after the deed is sold, whether you will earn interest on the premium is a fair question and one you need to check before bidding. Never be afraid to ask questions before the auction. It is the only way you are going to make sure you have all of the facts straight and be completely aware of all of the small, miscellaneous costs that may also be involved in buying tax liens from this particular county.

If the auction is being conducted by an outside auction company instead of the county directly, there may also be a *bidder's premium* that is attached to the bid. Usually about 10 percent, this is the commission that the auction company earns on the sale. Check the rules carefully to make sure you know what the total is going to be after you are through bidding.

## Bidding Down Ownership

With the *bidding down ownership* method, the winning bidder is the one who is willing to accept the least percentage of ownership in the property. This is not a frequently used method, and certainly not preferred by us as investors.

## Bidding Down Interest

Used by several states including Florida, the *bidding down interest* method requires bidders to compete for the lowest interest rate they are willing to accept on the lien. Bidders cannot bid a rate that is higher than the state-sanctioned rate, and the winning bidder is the one who is left standing with the lowest interest rate. I have seen these go down to 3 or 4 percent or lower at times, but only when the investor knows he is in a likely position to actually proceed with a foreclosure action to get the actual property. Otherwise, the investment wouldn't make much sense.

In these types of auctions, the delinquent property owner must still pay the statutory rate, but the local government will get to keep the difference as a premium. Sometimes the overage or *surplus* may be able to be claimed by the property owner down the road.

There are certain jurisdictions where the winner of a tax lien is guaranteed the right to any future tax liens on that property at full value. Because of this I have seen people bid a tax lien down to zero percent interest because they know there are two other tax liens on the property for subsequent years, and when they average the interest they will receive on all three liens together, it is still a very good investment. This is not something I recommend for the novice investor. You really need to have your facts and math right before you take on this type of investment.

## Lottery or Rotational Bidding

This bidding method identifies the first bidder (which is determined by a lottery or by the order of registration), and offers that bidder the first right of refusal on the current parcel up for bid. This means that a property is presented to that bidder first, and if the bidder chooses not to purchase that lien, then the same property is offered to the second bidder, and so on until the lien is either purchased or receives no bids. The catch to this method is that you may never know what property you'll have a chance to purchase because you have no control beyond accepting or declining the property that comes up when it happens to be your turn in the bidding rotation.

Think of this as a pot-luck auction. You do your research and go into the auction knowing which 10 properties you want to bid on. After getting to the auction you find out you are number one on the list of 30 people who get to bid. You figure you're all set. Well, not really. Because the first property that comes up for bidding may be one you have absolutely no interest in at all. So you pass on it and it goes on down the line. Now the second property comes up for bid. It's one that you really want. However, the bidding for that property starts with whoever is second in line. You have moved to the end of the list, so everyone in the room would have to pass on it before you even have a chance to make an offer. Theoretically, the remaining tax liens you came to purchase could come up for auction, and you never get to bid on any of them because the bid never makes it back to your position in line.

This type of auction is slow and frustrating, so I tend to avoid these. Fortunately, there aren't many of them around, and they are typically used only in smaller jurisdictions.

### First Come, First Served

*First come, first served* means just that. The first bid received that's in the full amount of the lien is the one that is accepted. Usually used for silent auctions or mail-in bidding, the actual determination of what constitutes *first* lies with the taxing authority. While each bid is usually date and time stamped upon receipt, the rules will be quite specific, and you want to follow them carefully. For bids that come in under *sealed bid* or via mail, the winning bid is simply the bid that is received first.

### Random Selection

This one is a little funky, and it's a lot like a lottery process. Under the *random selection method,* the bidding process is typically conducted using computer software and displayed on a screen. Names of investors are entered into the software and drawn by random computer selection, and then that investor is allowed to pick the parcel of his or her choice. In some smaller and more rural jurisdictions, random selection may mean a process as simple as picking names out of a hat. It really is amusing to see all of the different ways counties come up with to settle very serious tax issues that have consequences for both the property owner and the entire population of the county.

## ONSITE AUCTION TIPS

Let's face it—attending an onsite auction is fun. The people, the atmosphere, the excitement, the bidding, and of course winning a bid or two. But there are some tricks to the trade that you need to know before you walk into an auction. Once you get to the auction site, here are a few *Chip Tips* to help make it a smooth auction experience.

First, get there early and get registered if you aren't already. Bidder numbers are usually assigned based on order of registration. If there was no advance registration, register early in case seating is based on bidder number.

If there is no assigned seating, arrive at the auction site early so you can secure a good seat up front. Being in the front half of the auction room makes it easier for the auctioneer to see you, and you avoid distractions behind you. Arriving early also gives you time to prepare yourself mentally, get organized, get all of your research materials out, and highlight key properties on your list.

Hiding in the back of the room as you might have done in your school days is not the way to make money at a tax auction. You want to be visible to the auctioneer. One of the last things you want to have happen is to make a bid on a piece of property and, because you were sitting in the back, behind a column, with your spreadsheet up in front of your face, the auctioneer never heard your bid and now it's too late.

You've done your homework on each property up for bid, and you know the maximum price you're willing to pay or the minimum interest you're willing to accept. Check the onsite auction list one more time for last minute deletions or changes. Most auctions will have an updated sale list available there onsite, but they tend to run out of copies. Another good reason to get there early.

Don't be shy! Talk to the people working the auction (without distracting them from their jobs), and interact with other people who are there to bid. Most times, a high-level official from the county will be in attendance and will make a good point of contact for future questions or issues with properties. Without being overly enthusiastic, get to know this person! He will most likely become your best friend for information on upcoming auctions and also on over-the-counter auctions that happen after this auction ends. We'll go into OTC auctions later on in this chapter.

Auctions are also a great place to meet investment partners and learn from local experienced pros. There will likely be a lot of Realtors, landlords, and local developers there. The audience will also include some of the current property owners who didn't pay their taxes, or even tenants trying to find out what's going on. The rest of the people will include nosy neighbors and curious bystanders who simply want to watch. Experience has shown that only 20 to 40 percent of the people who attend will actually bid on anything. I have even received offers from other investors right there at the auction after I won the bid!

As a side note, if this is a tax deed auction and the tenants who are currently occupying the property are present, go and talk to them! Try to find out if they are planning to bid on the property, if you can. If not, find out as much as you can about the condition of the property to determine if the research and numbers you crunched beforehand will actually work. And lastly, if you do win the auction, then you can immediately speak with them about either staying in the property as tenants and paying you rent, or possibly doing a lease option and/or buying the property from you. You could have this property bought and sold without ever leaving the room!

As the auction gets ready to start, the auctioneer will explain the process and the rules. Listen carefully, and make sure to ask questions if something isn't quite clear. The auctioneer will then review any last-minute changes or deletions of auction items. Remember, most counties will err on the side of caution, and will allow property owners to pay their taxes and redeem the parcel right up until auction time. In the case of tax deeds, I have seen many parcels withdrawn at the last minute due to a possible legal glitch, so they really are trying to protect themselves and the previous owners and give them every opportunity to fix the situation before the sale. I had one property that I had bid on and won cancelled 15 minutes after the sale, since the owner had walked up and paid his taxes. In those cases, I am glad the owners are able to keep the property.

This is another reason why you must do your research and go into the auction with a list of properties you feel comfortable bidding on. Going to an auction and wanting to bid on only two or three properties is a waste of your time and money. The odds are that one of those properties will end up not being available for one reason or another, and the other two will go for bids higher than you were willing to pay. Think of it as making up a long shopping list and then running out to the store every day to buy one item on the list. That doesn't make any sense. Better to pick up everything you want at once.

So now it's auction time. Remember that good properties may sell for far more than the base bid, so again: know your maximums and minimums and stick to them. The auction is not the time to experiment or make hasty decisions that you may come to regret later. Go into it with the confidence of knowing exactly what you want to accomplish. If you are nervous or have doubts, bring a friend or someone experienced in bidding at auctions with you to help you with the bidding.

Avoid any and all diversions. Don't get distracted by fellow bidders, commotion in the room, or your cell phone (which should be off!). The pace at an auction, particularly a heavily attended auction, can be speedy at times, and you need to be focused and aware of what's happening. Otherwise, you risk losing track of the properties in which you're interested.

Recently I witnessed a woman who was texting and bidding at the same time. You have to wonder if she really ended up making the bids she intended to, or missed an opportunity because she was checking e-mail. With all her texting back and forth, it was distracting to everyone around her who was bidding as well. The last thing you want to do is get distracted, so if you are next to someone who is causing you to lose your focus—move! Also, don't be your worst enemy; wait until you are through bidding before you start checking your text messages!

---

**CHIP TIP:** Don't be the first bidder. Wait for others to bid, then enter after the initial bidding slows down. This eliminates nonserious competition.

---

Do not appear overanxious, or another interested party may drive up the bid on you. While the auction company won't use plants to drive up a bid, there may be other disgruntled parties there who are trying to make a point. I attended one auction once where two brothers and a sister were bidding against each other on their father's property. He had passed away, and the taxes didn't get paid. It got pretty heated, and emotions took over. You don't want to get involved in their games, so stay focused.

Be especially wary if the property owner is there to bid on one of the liens you are interested in. He or she may have one of several motives for being there. They could possibly have failed in their attempt to redeem the tax lien and now are willing to pay any price to keep the home. Or even worse, they could be there simply to make sure whoever does buy the lien pays the most possible for it.

To make it even more confusing, there may be other auctions going on at the same time. There might be mechanic liens being auctioned, recovered stolen property, foreclosure auctions—who knows. Make sure to pay attention to why you are there and what you are bidding on.

Just as you would for any important business transaction, meeting, or conference, come prepared with pens, paper, calculator, highlighter, and so on. These items will keep you organized and ensure you have what you need when you need it. Highlight the parcels you are interested in, and make sure that the printing is large enough to read easily. You don't want to be fumbling for glasses in the middle of the bidding.

Don't stand when you bid, but make sure that the auctioneer can see you clearly. Don't be afraid that if you brush back your hair they will count that as a bid. That may look funny on TV, but in reality, they will confirm that you are truly placing a bid before proceeding.

Another common myth is that you won't be able to understand the auctioneer. Most do not use the fast double-talk approach, and you'll pick up on their bid process quickly. If at any time you are not sure what the bid amount is, or if you are currently the high bidder—*ask*! Don't lose out on a bid because you weren't sure who was saying what.

## ONLINE AUCTIONS—BIDDING IN YOUR PAJAMAS!

Since the invention of eBay, people have been enamored with the ease, flexibility, and fun of participating in auctions online. Participating in an online tax sale auction allows you to bid without having to attend in person, and in fact allows you to attend from anywhere in the world. I have several students and clients who are located in many different countries, and they love these types of auctions. And yes, since no one was watching, I have even attended auctions in my pajamas!

To participate, you will of course need a computer and access to the Internet. For international bidders, you will also have to have the ability to pay for your winning bids in US dollars, and most likely may need to provide a US address as a point of contact. This can be established very quickly by contracting with a designated or resident agent. It is not always necessary, but it's worthwhile to establish if you plan on doing a lot of investing.

You will need to preregister at the county or auction company website and follow the step-by-step instructions. Many online auctions require the preregistration x-number of days in advance, and they may require a deposit placed in advance as well. Check the rules carefully, as deposit requirements can vary widely. For extremely high-value parcels, they may even require what is known as a *performance bond* to accompany your right to bid.

Some online auctions base the deposit on anticipated bids, and they require the bidder to make a 5 to 10 percent bidding payment via ACH payment, wire transfer, cashier's check, or money order, so again—check the county where you are bidding for the exact procedure and deposit amount. The day of the sale is not the time to start asking questions about these details.

As with onsite auctions, each property is given a file number and auctioned according to the order of the numbers. If there are many parcels, then they may be broken down into lots and sold at different staggered times or even on different dates. For online auctions, primarily the premium bidding method is used, and the property is simply sold to the highest bidder.

Even though there are times and deadlines on some online auction sites such as Bid4Assets.com, they use an overtime clock to extend the bidding for five minutes after the last bid is received. This makes sure that no bids are left on the table, but it can extend the auction for quite some time. I'm not a big fan of this, as I have seen auctions extended for 30 to 60 minutes as people continued to bid.

While you will be able to monitor the bidding activity, and even the amounts bid, the bidder names will generally remain confidential, or the auction may use a coded name to identify the current winning bidder. Make sure to constantly refresh your computer screen so that you can track the progression of the bids.

For areas that use bid down methods, the online auction site might use proxy bidding. This means that the auction software will automatically use the bid down interest method by searching for the lowest interest rate bid and then bidding automatically 1 percent lower until the lowest rate that the county is willing to accept is received. If there is a tie bid, then the auction software will randomly choose the winner. Don't give up. Remember the old cliché: "If at first you don't succeed, try, try again." If you keep at it long enough, eventually you will be successful.

If you are a successful bidder, you will need to remit the balance of the payment by using the ACH payment method or whatever payment method the county requires within the time specified by the county. Typically, payments must be made in full by the end of the auction or by the end of the following business day.

If you were not the winning bidder, then any money that you deposited will be refunded to you after the auction. Also, be forewarned—if you do not pay the balance on time, your deposit may be forfeited, your bid cancelled, and your bidding privileges permanently revoked by the county.

## ONLINE AUCTION STRATEGIES

Online auctions can be convenient and fun to participate in, but there are some strategies you need to follow in order to make them successful. Here are some basic tips to help you with your online bidding.

- Make sure to register with the site, and use your special e-mail that you set up just for your auction communications.
- Do not use your real name, company name, or a geographic location as your codename for bidding on properties. Stay as anonymous as possible while bidding online.
- Try out *practice auctions* in advance to get the feel for how it works. SRI has a great sample online auction site (see the 101 online resource listings).
- Make sure you are aware of the correct time zone when bidding. You may think a bid ends at 3:00 PM, when it really ended at noon your time.

- Stay logged-in during the bidding process if it ends within a few hours. If you are kicked out, or logged off, you may not see any bid changes, and logging back in may cause you to miss a deadline.
- Make sure it's a *real* tax sale auction, and only participate in online auctions that are designated and certified by the county as official. There are a lot of third-party sites that claim to be auctioning off tax foreclosed property, but you're not buying what you think you are.
- Even on sites like Bid4Assets, be careful to be sure the listing is for a tax sale. They list many different types of properties, and it can be easy to get them confused.
- If possible, download the list of liens/properties in advance and track updates.

When you are bidding, keep your cell phone, radio, or television off and avoid any other noise so you are not distracted. It's too easy for the kids, dog, or dinner to steal your attention, and you end up missing a bid notification or status change.

Another part of not being distracted is making sure all of your information is printed out and sitting in front of you, just as if you were physically sitting at the auction. Don't assume that the spreadsheets you created on your computer will be easy to pull up during the auction to get any information you may need. While you are busy minimizing the auction screen to look at your spreadsheet, the auction is still going on! Bids may be coming in and the auction could even close while you're looking at something else on your computer.

Also, computer files tend to get accidentally deleted when people are trying to do things fast and under stress. You may think you can just pop open your spreadsheet, get your information, and pop back into the auction in a flash, except you don't realize you accidentally deleted or saved the spreadsheet to a different folder on your computer when you clicked off of it. Now you go back to check on it, and it's gone! Not only have you possibly lost out on this auction, but while you are trying to recover your data, you could be losing out on all of the other auctions happening online.

Moral of the story, have all of your research printed out and organized on your desk. The only screen that should be up on your computer monitor during the entire auction is the auction itself.

## Advantages and Disadvantages

The biggest advantages of online auctions are that they are convenient because you do not have to physically attend the auction, thus saving you time and travel expenses. You also have a larger selection of liens/properties to choose from since you are not limited to your immediate geographic area. You are also not distracted by other bidders when you bid online, and you can work from the comfort of your own home or office.

On the other hand, you do not get to evaluate your competition or participate in the excitement of the bidding. It's also a lot easier to participate, so the competition can be greater and final bids higher than expected. There tend to be more novice bidders and investors who participate in an online auction, so you need to watch your maximum bids carefully and stick to them.

Another disadvantage is that online auctions can tend to last for days. This allows greater participation, but doesn't allow you the small window of opportunity to quickly grab the deal.

There is a list of some of the more established online auction sites in the back of this book, or you can find updated links and information for free on the Zero Risk Real Estate Resource Center at: www.ZeroRiskRealEstate .com/Bonus.

## CANCELLING YOUR BID

So what happens if you make a mistake? Simply walking away and not paying is not the right move, believe me. At an auction I attended a few years back, a man bid on a piece of property and then later realized he had bid on the wrong one. Instead of trying to correct it, he simply walked out of the building and never looked back.

Since there was not a deposit required, he didn't lose any money, but he lost a lot more. First, he will be banned from participating in any future auctions. Second, if there was any loss or expense in the resale of that item, the county could have come back and tried to collect it from him. And third—he just looked plain stupid for not fixing the problem right then and there.

Contrast that with an auction I attended in northern Michigan last year, where a bidder did the same thing but realized the mistake before the auction was over. The auctioneer simply announced that that parcel would be reopened for bidding, and it ended up selling for about the same price. He could do that since all the participants in the auction were still there.

Here's the bottom line: if you make a mistake when you are at an onsite auction, then tell someone right away and they will probably get it fixed. If you are on an online auction, there may not be any recourse after the bidding has ended, and you may lose any deposit you had submitted. That is another reason to make sure you are not distracted during the auction.

However, if you really do screw up an online auction, there is normally a phone number on the auction website you can call. Don't wait! Call that number immediately, identify yourself, and answer any security questions you may have had to create when you registered, and see if anyone can fix the problem before the auction is over.

## OVER-THE-COUNTER BARGAINS

So what if the auction is over and there are parcels left that didn't receive a bid? Or what if someone did screw up, and it wasn't caught until after the auction had ended? These parcels may still be available!

Be alert at the auction, and always stay until the end. If parcels are not paid for when due, it invalidates that auction item, and it may come up later in the day. Unpaid or unsold tax sale items can become available as what is known as an OTC (over-the-counter) or Assignment Certificates within a few days. Just because a parcel didn't sell doesn't mean the county doesn't still want to sell it.

In some cases, the county may hold what is known as a *cleanup auction* to sell these remaining items. At the cleanup sale, the minimum bids are usually eliminated or drastically reduced just to get them off the county books. In Indiana, these are known as *Commissioner Certificate* sales, and on those, the rate of return on a redemption actually goes up to 30 percent! I'll talk more about those in Chapter 8.

If it was an onsite sale, you can obtain a list of these OTC liens/properties directly from the county after an auction has taken place. For online auctions, they may simply relist the items at a later date.

These OTC liens are like going to the store and buying yesterday's bread. It isn't as if the bread has suddenly gone bad and has no value, it's just that no one actually bought it the day it was made. So because of this, the store sells it at a huge discount to make sure they don't get stuck with it. The lien you buy a few days after the auction is still just as valid as the day it went up for sale. You have all of the same rights and privileges regarding that lien. Except now, the county is afraid they may get stuck with it, so sometimes they are willing to sell it to you at a deep discount.

Buying OTCs directly from the county offers a number of distinct advantages. This is one of the best strategies available, so make sure you spend some time researching OTC properties. Here are some advantages.

- Since the auction is over, there is no more competition and therefore no more bidding.
- You are free to buy the property directly from the county without having to jostle for position, and can do it through the mail or over the phone.

- These properties are sold on a first come, first serve basis.
- You will get the maximum allowable interest rate at the minimum bid price every time.

Another great benefit is that the redemption clock started ticking at the time the property went up for sale, so you may be able to purchase a property that is nearing the end of its redemption period. This is particularly attractive if you're buying a lien and are interested in acquiring the property itself. You may be in a position to foreclose shortly after your purchase.

With OTCs, you are not tied to an auction sale date. In other words, once you've determined the states that allow over-the-counter sales, you can research available properties at your leisure, invest whenever you're ready and whenever you have the funding, and you don't have to wait for an auction date or feel pressured because the date is imminent. It's much more relaxed. But be careful—there may be a very valid reason that the property didn't sell the first time, so recheck your research thoroughly.

## PAYING FOR YOUR WINNING BID

Once the auction is over, it's time to pay for your winning bids. If you made any kind of advance deposit, this is subtracted from the total amount and you are left with the balance due.

Of course, you need to check your balance carefully. There may be premiums or fees added, a recording or processing fee, or even a tax. Make sure that you understand the breakdown, and ask for clarification if the amounts are coded instead of spelled out.

Make sure that your name, address, and contact information are correct on the form. In most cases, the name listed is the name in which the lien certificate or tax deed will be issued. So if you want it in a company name, make sure that is what is on there.

Almost every auction will require you to pay immediately following the conclusion of the auction. In a few cases, I've seen where you have to pay immediately after you bid! In other cases, the policy is that funds have to be received by 5:00 PM that day.

---

**CHIP TIP:** If you make a bid and do not complete payment, don't ever plan on returning to that county! You will be banned from future auctions.

For online auctions, be prepared to wire the funds into a special account within 24 to 48 hours. Again, it pays to check their payment policies in advance of the auction so you are prepared.

Virtually no live auctions allow you to pay with a personal or business check (although you can use these for many OTC or Assignment Certificates). Yet some, like those here in Michigan, require that you bring a $1,000 certified check, and the balance can be paid using a personal or company check.

Some auctions even allow credit cards to be used, but you may have to pay a premium to them in order to cover the credit card expense. Know the rules so that you will be ready.

In most cases, for onsite auctions you will be required to pay with cash or a cashier's check at the end of the auction. Since you don't know exactly how much you are going to end up bidding, or how many properties you might win, figuring this out can be a little challenging. One good trick is to have several different denominations of cashier's checks made out to yourself so you can put them together to pay various amounts. Then carry only a few hundred dollars in cash to make up the difference. For example, if I think I will end up bidding in the $10,000 range, I might bring nine cashier's checks for $1,000, one for $500, and the balance in cash. For security reasons, *don't bring thousands of dollars in cash with you.* I have seen people walk in with a backpack full of cash, and several people follow them out when they leave.

Tax sales are held every single day all across the country, and there are many investors who take part in auctions a couple of times a month either onsite or online. Once you've got the hang of it, all you need to do is simply rinse and repeat! But now that you've got the winning bid, let's take a look at how to protect the investment you just made.

# PROTECTING YOUR INVESTMENT

*The difference between death and taxes is that death doesn't get worse every time Congress meets.*

—Will Rogers

**W**OW! It's over and you had the winning bid! Congratulations—you now own a tax lien or maybe even a new property! Now that you have purchased your new investment, you need to take steps to ensure you are properly protecting it and maximizing its potential. The steps you need to take to protect yourself are sometimes very different, depending on whether you purchased a tax lien or a tax deed. In each of the steps I speak about below, I will outline these differences and make sure you have all of the information you need to keep your investment safe.

Of course, since you did your homework and due diligence, you know you've secured a good investment, and one that we consider *Zero Risk*. You learned that not all properties are created equal, and by eliminating the ones that may have potential built-in risks such as bad locations, low value ratios, or environmental problems, you are already one big step ahead of your competition. Even though you are not able to predict whether or not your property will appreciate in value and how economic factors will affect your property in the future, you have minimized the risks that are under your control, and have a built-in return on your investment.

In this chapter, we're going to take a close look at what steps you need to take to protect your interest in your new investment, insurance and maintenance concerns to be aware of, and of course the ultimate question—what if the tax lien doesn't get redeemed?

## WHAT TO DO FIRST

If you haven't already done so, the first thing you need to do is check your receipt and paperwork to match your purchases to the right parcels. Check the PID, also known as a *PIN*, but both are the number that the county uses to identify that particular piece of property, legal description, and auction lot numbers to be sure that they all correspond to your purchase, including the total amount paid. Mistakes have been known to happen, and the quicker they're caught, the easier they are to fix.

This receipt is sometimes the only thing you will get to substantiate your purchase, so protect it. In other transactions, you will be sent an actual tax certificate for your records, which then needs to be returned if and when redemption takes place. Other times, these certificates aren't needed and make great paper airplanes.

In the case of a tax deed, shortly after the sale, you will either receive a tax deed in *recordable* form, or the county will record the document for you. If it is sent to you in recordable form, then it is your responsibility to take the deed down to the County Clerk's office and have it recorded. There is normally a small recording fee you must pay to the county (around $8 to $10 a page).

Whether you record the deed yourself or the county records it for you, it will be mailed to you about 15 to 30 days after it's been officially registered and recorded in the County Recorder's office, but don't be surprised if it takes some counties a little longer. To help speed up the process, you should also send a self-addressed, stamped envelope to the clerk along with the deed you want to have recorded. While this is not mandatory, I have found it greatly reduces the chance of the document getting lost or not making its way back in a timely manner. In order to minimize your risks, make sure that you follow the state law procedures on what happens after your purchase.

For tax liens, there is next to nothing that you have to do, but for tax deeds it's a different story. The rules may vary from state to state, but the following are typically the next steps to take.

## Record Certificate

Recording the certificate is generally necessary only for tax deed purchases, but again—at some point after the sale, you will receive some form of proof of your purchase in either recordable format, meaning that it meets the county requirements to be legally recorded in the county records, or stamped by the clerk showing it already has been recorded.

If it is sent to you unrecorded, it may be in the form of a simple one-page certificate that says "Tax Deed" at the top, but *check it carefully!* Make sure that the property information is correct (especially the parcel ID# and legal description), and that your contact information is correct. I have caught errors in mixed-up legal descriptions, or copies that were sent to me instead of the originals. You need to have an original signature on the document in order to record it, and the document must also normally have been notarized and witnessed by independent third parties. Make sure nothing is wrong or missing from the document.

 Check the legal description carefully for accuracy! It's easier to fix *before* the document is recorded.

Checking the legal description is critical. The easiest way to do this yourself is to have a copy in hand of the current deed on the property to compare it to. If the description is off at all, then contact the county and get it fixed immediately, especially if it is before the document is going off for recording.

I once had a student who bought a tax lien on a condominium unit. The legal description, which was several paragraphs long, was off by only one number. Instead of saying unit 1505, it said unit 505. Well, this was a high-rise condominium, and unit 505 was worth about $125,000 less than unit 1505. If this deed had been recorded and had gone to the foreclosure stage without anyone catching the mistake, it would have been a massive pain and expense to fix. My student would have hired an attorney to do all of the paperwork to foreclose, only to find out that it had been all wrong! Then he would have needed the attorney to start a new action to be brought to the court to have the legal description corrected before he could restart the foreclosure. It is much easier and cheaper to fix this kind of mistake when it first happens, so be sure to check all of your paperwork carefully.

On the tax lien side, if they actually issue you a certificate, you may need to record it with the county clerk and pay the necessary filing fees, but check. Keep copies, and if you mail it in, always send it by certified mail so that you can track their receiving it on the other end. I know it's hard to believe, but county departments can lose documents once in a while. In states that just send you a receipt, recording the certificate is usually not needed or required.

I once sent a tax deed in for recording in Orange County, Florida. Please understand, I am not picking on this particular county, since these mistakes can happen anywhere. I waited a month for my self-addressed envelope to arrive. Finally I called the clerk's office and inquired about my deed. After a few minutes of waiting for them to look it up, they told me it was just sent back to me by mail. When I asked what the problem with it was, they told me that the check I sent along with the deed to pay for the recording was off by 15 cents. Because of this they had to mail it back to me so I could issue them a new check. Now, understand that the check I sent them was *over* by 15 cents, not short. Most counties across the country will mail you back an overage check along with the copy of the deed if you overpaid for the recording. However, there are some who simply will not record your document if you are off by one penny. The moral of the story is: to prevent delays, always check with the clerk's office about the correct recording fees before you mail anything out.

Another thing to remember, as I stated above, is always keep a photocopy for yourself of any document you send off to the county clerk to have recorded. In larger counties where there is a backlog of documents to be recorded, it is not uncommon for things to get misplaced. Having a photocopy in your possession gives you some hard evidence to prove that the document in fact existed.

## Notification

Check carefully. A couple of states actually require that you notify the property owner upon purchase of the lien. Most do not, as the taxes are still paid to the county during the redemption period. If you do have to send any type of notice, make sure you send it by certified mail with return receipt requested. Keep the original return receipts you get back in the mail in a file for that property. You will need this proof later on if you go to foreclose. When in doubt about the notification requirements, check with a real estate attorney.

## Pay Taxes

When you purchased the tax deed, the delinquent taxes on the property were for a previous year, so there may be current taxes you will need to pay as part of your purchase. The previous year's taxes are wiped out, but it may be a condition of the sale that you have to pay the next or current tax bill by a certain date.

In some states, such as Texas, you are not allowed to bid until you file a certification that you are not personally delinquent on any other property taxes on parcels that you may own in that state. This is to prevent a type of tax lien scam that involves buying properties that have delinquent taxes owed and intentionally not bringing the taxes current. Instead, what these people do is rent the home out, collect the payments, not pay the county, and wait for the county to go ahead and foreclose on the tax lien. The county conducts the auction just as we've discussed, and any overage they receive for the tax lien is paid to the last owner of record on the property, which would be them. So they end up getting paid for any additional monies the county may collect on their own property's tax lien, all the while ignoring their obligation and getting paid to rent the property out! Not only is this unethical but, as you can see, states are getting wise to this and cracking down, and the potential for prosecution for criminal fraud exists. Once again, always consult with a real estate or tax attorney before engaging in any type of conduct that seems suspect.

# PROTECTING YOUR TAX LIEN INTEREST

Tax lien investments are pretty easy to babysit. There is really nothing special you have to do to protect your interest except track the redemption dates. If and when the tax lien redeems, the county will simply send you a check. If it doesn't redeem, then you may have to go through the foreclosure process to secure your interest, but that's discussed in a later section. You don't *have* to foreclose, but if you did your research correctly, you'll want to in order to increase your profits. This is why we call it the *Zero Risk* system. You make money no matter what happens to your tax lien.

Make sure you do keep good records of your tax lien purchases though. Keep a simple filing system with a separate file for each property by its address. You will have to have a tickler system in place to remind you of important dates. Any standard calendar software will work. You don't need to spend a lot of money for fancy software to get this done. Google has a calendar feature that does a fine job of keeping track of all of these dates for you and sending you e-mails and pop-ups when certain events are due. And it's free! Remember, the county will not remind you of anything—redemption dates, filing dates, foreclosure windows, other tax liens, or any other required legal actions—so make sure you are organized and keep these dates and events backed up and secure.

As a lien holder of record, you will be required to be notified of any actions involving the property. I've received notifications of mortgage foreclosures, housing violations, lawn or snow removal violations, mechanic's liens, and even notices of condemnations. Something else to be aware of is homeowner's association violations that occur on the property. This is only a concern if you purchase a property that is part of an HOA, but it can cause some serious fines to rack up against the property, and these notices can look a little scary when you get them. A notice that says the property is being fined $100 a day until the driveway is repainted can add up.

Don't panic, you are still in what is called a *superior* and secure title position relative to any new actions, but the county is still required to notify you. That's another good reason to double-check that your mailing address is correct, and notify the county if it changes.

## PROTECTING YOUR TAX DEED

If you acquired the property as a tax deed, you now own it. This is a whole different ballgame, and now you need to take specific actions to protect yourself and your position. It is a good idea to make sure that you have homeowner's insurance lined up and placed on the property right away, even if it is still occupied by the previous owner or if there is a continued right of redemption. As the owner, you are now going to be liable for any losses incurred from that point forward. You also want to make sure you have personal liability insurance on the property included in your homeowner's policy. The reason for this is you are most likely going to be showing the property to potential buyers and Realtors, and you will be hiring contractors to do work on the property. The last thing you need is for someone to whom you gave access to the property to fall and hurt themselves and then try to collect damages from you personally.

If the property is vacant, make sure to secure it with new locks and to board up windows if necessary to eliminate the chance of vandalism or other unwanted activity (vacant properties seem to be a magnet for the local teenagers to go to and throw wild parties). Insurance may be difficult or impossible to get on a vacant or abandoned property, but check around with multiple agents to find out your options.

If the property is occupied, you may have to initiate a legal court proceeding known as an *eviction action* to remove the occupants. I'll cover this in more detail in the next chapter, but this can take some time in certain states, so consult an attorney to make sure you do it correctly.

If there are obvious safety or health issues with the property, such as a severe roof leak, major hole in the yard, missing steps on a stairway, exposed live electrical wires, or similar situations, these need to be addressed right away. The last thing you want to happen is to be sitting in your living room and turn on the evening news only to see that a large crowd has gathered on your property's lawn because a child fell into an old well you did not secure with a cover, and now they can't get the child out! If you are not a handyman, then get on Craigslist.org or Angieslist.com and get someone out to the property to fix all these problems immediately.

One of the first things I try to do when I buy a property through a tax deed is to go to the property to meet the neighbors. In most cases, they'll be glad that someone new is taking over, and you can learn some interesting history about the property. This is also known as *gossip*, but it's a great way to find out why the property went into default in the first place and whether there are any hidden defects in the property. I once had a neighbor tell me how "they always had plumbers coming in and out of there." Well, it turned out there was a series of steady leaks in a basement pipe. There would have been no way for me to know about this until I turned the water on and saw my basement flooded, along with getting a huge water bill from the city! Apparently the previous owners kept paying different plumbers to come back and try to fix the leaks, thinking the previous plumber they hired hadn't done a good enough job. Once I determined where the pipe with the leaks was located in the house, I just had a contractor replace the entire section of piping for a few hundred dollars, and I knew I would not have to deal with it again.

Also, not long ago, I obtained a property through a tax sale in Indiana on a vacant home that was in the middle of a total rehabilitation project. It looked like someone had just up and walked away one day. I met the neighbor across the street, who explained that the former owner was a young single man who had been killed by a drunk driver in a car accident late one night. His girlfriend couldn't redeem the property since she was not on title, and there was no immediate family, so the property renovations were never completed and the property went into the tax sale.

Best part, though, is that I ended up selling the property to that neighbor, who then fixed it up as a rental property. Another win–win, and a nice profit on my side of the ledger. So yes, sometimes it does pay to gossip.

## INSURANCE AND PROPERTY MAINTENANCE

As I mentioned, insurance can be difficult to get on a vacant property. Homeowners looking to insure a vacant home typically have two options: buying an endorsement to their existing homeowner's policy or purchasing a separate vacant-home insurance policy. But if you cannot get insurance, then make sure that you have a personal *blanket liability* policy in place to protect you in case something nasty happens at the property. This will cover you for anything and everything that may happen. As I discussed earlier, all it takes is a quick slip-n-fall accident on a snow-covered sidewalk to ruin your day, or month, or year. Of course, another way to provide some protection is through holding your investments in a separate entity such as an LLC, which we discuss in Chapter 8.

Basic insurance is fine. You do not need comprehensive coverage, as you only have a few thousand dollars invested. If you spent $5,000 on a tax deed for a property worth $120,000, the most you can truly lose is still $5,000. It's a gamble, but discuss the options with your insurance agent.

However, the upside to getting comprehensive coverage is you are insured for the full value of the property. So if something like a storm hits the house and severely damages the property, the insurance company will write you a check for the total amount of the damages up to the value of the property and not just for the $5,000 in value you insured. For example, if a storm came and blew the roof away and did $25,000 in damage to the property, you would get a check for $25,000 instead of just a break–even check for $5,000.

You don't have to fix the roof with that money. You can sell the house *as is* to another investor for, say, $10,000. Let's say the house is worth $100,000 with the roof fixed, so the other investor knows he can spend a total of $35,000 to buy the property and have it repaired, and when he's done he will have a property worth $100,000, so it's a good deal for him. It's also a good deal for you because you took your original $5,000 investment and collected $25,000 from the insurance company and $10,000 from another investor for a grand total of $30,000 in profit.

While these types of scenarios are rare (although depending on what part of the country your property is in, it may not be as rare as others), it shows how even in the face of having the property you purchased by tax deed destroyed, you can still come out with a killer profit using the *Zero Risk* system.

---

**CHIP TIP:** Use an insurance agent who is local to the property, and interview several agents before deciding on your coverage. Costs and policies will vary widely.

---

If you just purchased the tax lien, you are not responsible for the maintenance of the property, although you may want to check it now and then to make sure there is not some significant change or deterioration going on. But this is rare.

As the new property owner through a tax deed, you *will* also be responsible for lawn care and snow removal. I like to hire a neighbor kid to take care of these things, since they will also keep an eye on the property for me and call me if something happens.

On a rare occasion, I have been notified of a property condemnation or housing violation hearing during the redemption period. This is a difficult situation, since you are not permitted to do anything to the property (including correcting any violations) as simply a tax lien holder. You have no ownership rights in the property and cannot even legally walk onto the property if it is still occupied. In these circumstances, you need to evaluate whether you want to proceed with your interest. In a couple of instances, I have simply let my tax lien interest expire without foreclosing to avoid liability for these future violations. I call it getting an education the hard way—you should call it learning from someone else's past experience! The old adage about "throwing good money after bad" does have its merits. In these rare instances it is better to take a small loss now than end up paying for a potential huge loss down the road.

## WHAT TO DO WHEN YOUR PROPERTY DOESN'T REDEEM

There is always a chance that you won't get paid on your tax lien certificate if the property owner (or lender) does not redeem the property and pay the taxes prior to the expiration of the redemption period. The odds are against it, since over 95 percent of tax liens (excluding vacant land) are redeemed. But if you did your research correctly, then this should be a windfall for you if it happens.

If you do find yourself in this position, then you may have to foreclose on the property. The term *foreclosure* means that the title to the property is now being taken away from the owner, and the person who forecloses is now the new property owner because the owner failed to meet their obligations. Not a fun process, at least not until you come out the other side with a full, complete, free-and-clear title to the property.

Still, taking title to any property through foreclosure is never a fun process. It probably goes without saying that this is not something you should tackle yourself. You need to consult with a real estate attorney to make sure you follow state statutes to the letter regarding foreclosure and quiet title procedures.

Now you know why I've dedicated the entire next chapter to this topic. Taking control of a property is part art and part legal maneuvers. But it also comes with some unexpected rewards.

# TAKING CONTROL OF YOUR PROPERTY

*Buying real estate is not only the best way, the quickest way, the safest way, but the only way to become wealthy.*

—Marshall Field

One of the most difficult parts of the tax lien or tax deed process is taking physical control of the property. When you purchase a tax lien, you need to keep in the back of your mind whether you want to own the property if the owner fails to redeem it. Each investment should be made with this very question in mind.

Owning property comes with certain responsibilities and, of course, some additional costs to maintain the property. If you are a little squeamish about foreclosures or having to evict someone, another route might be to simply sell or assign your interest over to another investor. If you want to maximize your profits on the deal, however, and there are former owners or tenants who are living at the property, then you may have to evict them.

In this chapter, we're going to dive into the foreclosure process from the investor's point of view. We will learn how to deal with the art of eviction, what to do when confronted by previous owners, and how to handle claims by other interested parties.

## DO YOU REALLY WANT TO OWN IT?

Things change. You may have gotten into a tax lien investment, and after several years you decided that the property was no longer attractive to you, or it didn't fit within your investment objectives. Maybe the property has a major defect or structural problem, or someone put in a landfill across the street. So the main question is—do you still really want to own it?

I hope that the answer is still yes. But if it's not, then you need to look at liquidating your position and recouping your investment. You are still at *Zero Risk* for a couple of reasons. First, your research determined that you were well protected in the value of your investment. Second, while it's not large or established, there is a market for matured tax lien certificates. This allows you to sell your interest to another investor who is experienced and interested in the foreclosure of your lien interest.

There are a couple of resources listed in this book's Appendix, or you can check out the Zero Risk Resource Center for ideas and links. One source where I have seen tax sale certificates sold is right on eBay! Just be aware that you may be giving up a huge profit potential, even on the seemingly redeemable situations.

Even if the thought of having to foreclose on someone's home makes you feel uneasy, you have to treat this as a business. You are not the one who did not pay the taxes that were owed on a piece of property. You are not the bad guy, and don't ever let anyone make you feel like you are. If you did not buy this tax lien or tax deed, someone else most likely would have (say, the person you were bidding against?). It's not as if by purchasing this lien you are now forcing these people out of their home. They will be leaving, whether you purchase the lien or not.

In fact, as you will see in some examples later in this chapter, there are many win-win scenarios for both you and the homeowner if you approach the situation correctly. You will learn how to be compassionate about people's hardship while still making money on your investment. But you are always going to run into the miserable person who blames the world for his problems, and who will act like you are the devil incarnate for having the nerve to actually want back the money you paid on his behalf! Never lose a night's sleep over this type of person. Sleep like a baby—and if you don't want to handle it, then hire someone to do it for you. Just don't walk away from a huge profit because someone "made you feel bad."

If you decide to move forward with full acquisition of the property, then you have three steps to complete and one decision to make. Here's your new list:

- Take full legal control of the property.
- Take full physical control of the property.
- Perform some rehab and/or clean-up work.
- Decide to either keep it, lease it, or sell it.

Getting legal control and getting physical control of the property are two completely different things, but they don't have to be difficult or excessively expensive. Ninety-nine percent of all the properties I've ever been involved with have needed some sort of repairs and clean-up work. It is, of course, possible to just sell the properties sight unseen in as-is condition, but you will be leaving a lot of money on the table if you take that approach.

I recently took back what is commonly referred to as a *hoarder house*. You know, the kind you see on cable TV, with stuff stashed so high inside that you can't even enter the house. In my hoarder house, it took five 50-yard dumpsters and a crew three days to get everything out of it. But even after spending $3,500 on the clean-up process, it increased the former selling price (in as-is condition) by about $15,000. I sold the house within a week once it was empty.

Something else to keep in mind: anything that is left in the home by the former owners or tenants is considered abandoned property. You take ownership of it when you take possession of the property. (Some jurisdictions require you to hold onto the property for 30 days and post a notice in the paper before taking possession, but either way, eventually it's yours.) Now, in the example I gave you, the house was literally filled with junk. But I have taken back houses that had some valuables inside. One house had a baby grand piano, another had a collection of antique dolls, and I even heard of someone finding a safe in the bedroom wall, and when they had a professional cut it open, they found some pretty valuable jewelry. And of course, you've heard stories of people finding money inside walls. Well, it does happen.

So why would people leave these things behind? Any number of reasons. They left in the middle of the night and simply forgot. The owner died and the house went to tax sale with these items still inside. The thing to remember is: double-check all of the closets, attic, and basement before you resell the property. You never know what additional profits your tax deed might yield!

The fourth item on the above list is really a personal decision based upon your long-term plans, but I am going to assume that, most of the time, your interest is in selling the property and cashing in. That's the entire purpose of Chapter 7!

# UNDERSTANDING THE FORECLOSURE PROCESS

Your first step is to get legal control of the property. How to do this is not the most fun topic, but it is one that we need to cover in detail. Just because you have a tax lien and it wasn't redeemed does not mean you automatically get legal possession of the property. In almost every case, you will have to file a petition with the county and/or the court to have the lien transferred over to a tax deed.

Remember: this is a process best handled by the pros. I strongly recommend that you consult an attorney when filing a foreclosure action, since many things can go wrong, and one slip-up could cost you a lot of time and money, especially if you have to start over.

When a property owner fails to reclaim the property during the redemption period, you have to foreclose on the property in order to get legal title. The term *foreclosure* means a lender takes title away from the owner as a consequence of the borrower's failure to make payments.

While this is a tough situation for all involved, there may be times when this is your only alternative, and you should be prepared accordingly. The critical components of a typical foreclosure are as follows.

You file a tax foreclosure or a *quiet title* action in the appropriate court in order to do what is called *perfecting* the tax deed, and have it legally declared that your title is superior to all others. The lawsuit and the summons are served on the property owner and anyone else who has a recorded interest in the property, including the mortgage company and any other lien holders.

Another common reason for seeking an action to quiet title is to clear up any possible lingering problems associated with property that has been conveyed by using a quitclaim deed. A quitclaim deed is used by many real estate investors as a way to transfer property without having to insure it against all liens and claims of interest. It basically ensures that the previous owner relinquishes all claims to the property, but does not necessarily pledge that the title is completely clear. Since the quitclaim deed does leave the door open for other former owners to claim an interest in the property, some means of protecting the interests of the current owner is necessary. That is where the quiet title comes in.

When property is purchased with the use of a quitclaim deed, the new owner usually moves forward with requesting a quiet title as soon as possible. Doing so provides the security of ownership that a quitclaim deed cannot provide. Once the quiet title is granted, the owner can be sure that the title is considered good and can proceed to make use of the property in any manner allowed by current laws. The property also becomes more valuable since any possibility of former liens or claims evaporates.

If the previous owner is deceased, then an additional step of publishing a legal notice in the newspaper may be required, but your attorney will handle this as part of the process.

Once the court determines that all the appropriate notices were provided to the interested parties, all the papers are in order, and all applicable redemption periods have expired, it will enter a judgment declaring that you now have title, free and clear, that is superior to all other interests. Congratulations—you now own property worth a great deal more than you paid for it!

 Make sure to provide a copy of this judgment to the title company. They will need it to insure the title for the next purchaser when you sell it.

Having this judgment in your possession can also save you money on closing costs when it comes time to sell the property. In many states, the seller of a property is required to pay for title insurance for the buyer because it is the standard practice of the jurisdiction. Title insurance rates are normally promulgated or regulated by the state, so they follow a fixed price depending on how much insurance is being given. For example, a state that charges $7 per $1,000 of insurance would collect $700 to insure a $100,000 sale. You would be responsible for paying this $700.

However, if you have your judgment of quiet title, then you can ask for what's called a *reissue rate*. This is a discounted rate for title insurance when the seller can provide recent certification of ownership. That $700 policy may now cost you only $500 with a reissue rate. You just made an extra $200 on your investment simply for keeping your paperwork organized.

As I mentioned, and I can't state this strongly enough, in order to initiate foreclosure and pursue this legal action, you will want to hire an attorney. In some cases, property owners may defend such lawsuits with the hope of maintaining their ownership, but this is unlikely, because if they have the money to fight the foreclosure action they wouldn't have lost the property in the first place. If you're not careful, this could lead to extensive and expensive litigation that could very well eat into the profits you hope to see from the transaction. I have never had a former owner come back and challenge my ownership at this point.

Most of these legal actions, however, are simple and straightforward without incident, but they can take anywhere from two to eight weeks. Find an attorney who specializes in these types of actions, and it should not cost more than $1,000 to $1,800 in most situations. Still, this is a small price to pay for protecting your interests and getting a true free and clear title that's insurable.

Almost all attorneys who specialize in foreclosures will give you a fixed price for proceeding with the action. It is critical you do this and negotiate the full, maximum cost of the foreclosure action with the attorney you hire. Some may require $500 up front, then another $500 to file the action, and then a maximum of another $500 if they have to appear in court. This is fine, because you still can determine what your maximum cost for the litigation will be.

 Always ask your attorney for a *fixed fee* arrangement for filing a foreclosure or quiet title action.

Do not hire an attorney who wants to bill you hourly to handle your foreclosure because your bill will be open-ended. You will have no control over how much this foreclosure will cost, and then you can't budget this into your total costs to acquire the property. I've seen people pay thousands of dollars to an attorney in billable hours and still not have clean title to the property. They end up firing that attorney and finding one who will finish the litigation for them at a fixed price. If you talk to an attorney who insists on billing you hourly, go talk with another attorney.

## THE COSTS OF FORECLOSURE AND POSSESSION

While the thought of having to initiate a foreclosure action seems daunting, it's really not as difficult as you might think. However, it is a process that needs to be done correctly, since any little mistake can cost you a great deal of time and money, and it may even force you to start over from scratch.

That being said, I will reiterate my point of finding a real estate attorney who can help you with this. I use one every single time, and I don't look at it as an expense but more of an investment in peace of mind. The process can vary greatly from state to state, but the objective is the same: making sure that you get legal and physical possession of the property.

To obtain legal possession from a tax lien position, you will likely incur initial expenses of between $400 to upwards of $2,500. This will depend on who has to be notified and through what channels. Legal postings can cost a lot, but the newspapers that run these postings seem to have a monopoly on the market. The court will only recognize the legality of the posting if you use one particular newspaper. I don't know why, because it is normally a business newspaper that only a few thousand people may read, while the local paper may be read by tens of thousands. But some things you just can't argue over, and you have to accept the system as the cost of doing business.

If you've received the property through a tax deed sale, then you may not have to foreclose at all, but be prepared for having to file a follow-up quiet title action. Do not search out and hire the biggest, baddest real estate attorney in town. They have a place and purpose, but this isn't it. Instead, locate a small firm or single attorney practice, but make sure they have a strong practice in real estate. You don't want a divorce attorney representing you. (Unless, of course, you didn't follow the steps I have laid out for you in my *Zero Risk* process, and have lost a ton of money, and now your wife wants a divorce.)

---

**CHIP TIP:** I find and hire attorneys in unfamiliar areas by placing a small ad on Craigslist. Some of my best attorneys have come by using this method.

You may need this attorney for not only the quiet title and foreclosure proceedings but also for evictions of tenants or former owners of the property, or other matters involving the use of the property such as easements, zoning, and maybe even sale of the property.

When it comes to gaining actual physical possession of the property, this is not the same as a landlord/tenant dispute. The process of eviction is typically much faster since there is no tenancy relationship, so there are no tenant's rights.

 WARNING: Do not enter the premises if it appears that someone is living there. You could be charged with trespassing or possibly end up with a baseball bat to your head. Make sure you clear the legal possession hurdles first.

## ADVERSE POSSESSION

You might also be able to take possession by what is known as *adverse possession*. Adverse possession means you acquire title to property because the owner has abandoned it and you've essentially taken control of and live on the property. There is also the possibility that you may have to defend yourself against a government condemnation or eminent domain action when the government decides they want to take private property and use it for a public land use. Having a contingency plan in mind is recommended if for some reason you end up taking possession of the property.

In general, legal conditions required by courts in order to rule in favor of adverse possession include:

1. **O**pen and notorious
2. **U**ninterrupted use for X number of years or more
3. **C**laim of right
4. **H**ostile to the owner's intent
5. Property taxes were paid by the adverse possessor

These requirements are sometimes known as *Ouch + Taxes*. If you meet the conditions, it may be possible for you to file a quiet title lawsuit establishing that you acquired title through adverse possession. There may be additional requirements and/or variations from jurisdiction to jurisdiction.

Remember that adverse possession means more than just dropping in now and then to do some general caretaking. You have to actually live on the property, which isn't always feasible if the property has been abandoned and possibly is in disrepair. I would never advise you to start investing a lot of repair money in a property that you don't clearly own.

Also, adverse possession is not an overnight type of thing. You can't just move into the house and then file an action with the court the next day. The U from ouch stands for uninterrupted use for a number of years. This can be anywhere from 2 to 20 years depending on your jurisdiction. Adverse possession is not the way to go if you want to take quick control of a piece of property.

As noted above, adverse possession varies based on state and local law, so always be sure to consult an attorney familiar with the laws in that state before you get too comfortable.

## EMINENT DOMAIN AND CONDEMNATION

The government has the power to take our property and use it for a public use. They can take all or a portion or even be entitled to an easement such as a utility easement. Each state regulates how the government can take private property and the procedures for doing so. However, they must give the property owner notice and an opportunity to contest the matter. Here is how the condemnation process typically works.

The government sends you a notice about why they want the property and identifies the name and type of public project they want to use the property for. Once the property is appraised, the fair market value will be determined. You have the right by law to be paid justly for the property if the government takes it away from you. The government will make an offer specifying the amount they are willing to pay you for the property. You can accept their offer or sue the government and litigate the matter by taking it to court.

A friend of mine acquired a home through buying a tax deed at a local county auction on a home that was located in a redevelopment area of his town. Part of the area was still blighted, and the other part was experiencing a boom of redevelopment. My friend's property was located on the border of the redeveloped area and that was one of the reasons why he decided to buy the tax deed, because he believed it would be a good investment. He was approached about two years later by the city, who said that they needed to take possession of the property because the city had decided to make a deal with a developer to build a small park and 60 senior condominium units. My friend was actually offered more than current fair market value and he decided to take the offer.

In this instance, the eminent domain was actually a financially rewarding event for him. I have also heard stories where the city takes private property from one owner only to give it to a neighbor. So be careful if you are involved in an eminent domain action, and be sure to investigate thoroughly the reasons why the city wants your property so you will be in the strongest bargaining position if they do approach you and want to acquire your property.

# THE ART OF EVICTION—OR NOT!

There will come a time in your new investing career when you purchase a tax deed or foreclose on a tax lien, and the property is occupied. This is both a good thing and a bad thing.

Before I explain the pros and cons, let me state that it is never my intent to put someone out on the street. I have gone out of my way at times to help people who were in a tough stretch as much as I could, but I did have to protect my investments at the same time.

I remember attending an auction a few years back, where a property came up for tax sale that I had not even looked at or considered purchasing. I did know the area so I was familiar with values, but I hadn't done any research on this one at all.

When the item came up for bid, the auctioneer stopped and indicated that someone wanted to make a statement before the sale of the home. In this case, it was the current tenant. He explained that they had lived there for the past six years, the owner had died, and no one had ever come to see them about the property since. He had been maintaining the home, and he hoped that whoever bought it would allow them to continue to live there. Oh—and one twist—his wife was on disability and receiving a steady income from the state.

Now I was interested. Not just from an investment standpoint, but from a human standpoint. Here was a family whose world was about to be upended, and it didn't need to be. I could purchase the property with an existing tenant and with the knowledge that they weren't going to go away. I bid on the property and ending up winning the bid for just a few thousand dollars. We did a few repairs and got the place looking good. That family still lives there to this day, and their payments come in every month like clockwork.

But it isn't always so pleasant. With an eviction, the intent is to receive the possession of the property as opposed to receiving ownership title to the property. But this too is a legal process, and when you evict a tenant or former owner, you must follow the laws of the state where the property is located in order to evict anyone who lives on your property.

The procedure is typically as follows.

- The required notice must be sent to the tenant or owner giving them time to move. Typically 30 to 90 days is the standard eviction notice time deadline, but I have seen the court set it as quickly as 10 days.
- If the person(s) you are evicting has not left by the required time period, then you will have to file a notice with the local court and legally serve the person(s) you are evicting.
- If they fight it, you and the person(s) you are trying to evict can go to arbitration, mediation, or have the court decide a solution.

- When you are granted the eviction, then you must pay the sheriff to evict the tenant. You are not legally allowed to physically remove the person(s) from your property.

Of course, there is a legal eviction, and then there's the practical eviction. Over the years, I've had to learn what I refer to as the *art of eviction*. When you do it right, it can have some real benefits.

First, try to visit the property and meet with the residents in person. If that's not possible, then mail a letter and leave a note on the door asking them to call you. A typical letter I might send is shown in Figure 5.1.

As you can see, I am trying to give them an opportunity to help solve the problem. Until I understand the situation, I can't help them. But they may be able to solve the problem in any number of ways. If they are former tenants of the previous owner, maybe they just didn't get along with him. They still might like to stay and rent from you, since you would represent new ownership.

One of my favorite tactics is to just sell them the property. I'm not big on being a landlord personally, but I enjoy collecting payments on a seller's mortgage note or on a land contract. You really have nothing to lose at that point, and everything to gain.

---

**CHIP TIP:** Actually pay the tenants a small amount to move out and clean up. A couple of hundred bucks may be enough to motivate them to get out.

---

If they don't want to stay and pay, then you have to negotiate them out. The best solution is to offer the tenant or former owner cash for keys, which will save you the unpleasant task of having to evict them. It might just be a matter of being unable to *physically* move out. I had one situation where I simply agreed to provide a U-Haul truck for the weekend. I dropped off the keys on Friday and told them I would pick up the truck on Monday. They not only moved out, but the house was clean when I showed up!

Sometimes, it just takes the legal system to scare them into action. There have been many times when my letters and door notes have gone unanswered, only to have the occupants show up at the court hearing and negotiate a last-minute deal with my attorney.

---

 Make sure your attorney continually tries to negotiate a settlement with the occupants. It will save you a lot of money in the long run.

## Figure 5.1
## Letter to Occupant

(date)

TO: Mr/Mrs Jones AND ALL OTHER OCCUPANTS

Re: 123 Main Street, City, State, Zip

My name is *(your name)* and you may be aware that I recently took title to this property.

I am a real estate investor and would like to offer you the opportunity to either purchase this house or continue living in it. While I am not aware of your current situation or any problems you may have had with the previous owner, I would like to get to know you and see if we can make a deal.

I am very familiar with creative financing and may know of a way for you to purchase the property from me—even if you currently have no cash or credit problems. I welcome the opportunity to discuss this with you as soon as possible. I can be reached at *(your phone number)*.

If I do not hear from you within the next several days, then I will be forced to bring a legal eviction action against you in order to retake possession of my property. However, I would much rather see if we can work something out together first. Keeping attorneys and the courts out of this will be cheaper for both of us.

Thank you, and I look forward to speaking with you!

(Your name)

(phone)

Note: This form can be downloaded electronically at www.ZeroRiskRealEstate.com/Bonus.

Regardless, in the end you have to be prepared to move forward and force them out. Fortunately, through the art of negotiation and going through the extra steps I've mentioned, my instances of physical eviction have been very limited.

However, not every landlord has learned the art of eviction, and sending the wrong letter can make the process extremely difficult. Here is a letter a tenant showed me after I had taken possession of her property through a tax sale. This letter was sent to her by the previous landlord.

> Dear (tenant),
>
> I believe you have emotional problems that I cannot deal with, such as arachnophobia, then it will be ants, then mice, then rats and who knows that else you will find wrong. I don't need a whiner or constant complainer, or a disruptive tenant. I have many hours in the apartment, cleaning, papering and painting and never found swarms of anything.
>
> You are a busy-body, running to the neighbors, who know nothing about how many tenants I have had in the past, and besides that it is none of your business, and I won't have a snoopy tenant on my premises. Now that you have made it your business, please leave.
>
> Please have your entire possession removed by (date). You have been given one week of free rent.
>
> Sincerely,
> (landlord)

This actually was a very nice lady who just wanted the place exterminated. She couldn't understand why this landlord was giving her such a hard time, and happened to ask the other tenants if they were having problems with bugs and if any of their apartments had ever been exterminated. It turned out they all were having problems and, since it didn't make sense just to exterminate one apartment, they approached the landlord to have the whole building done. Behind the scenes, the landlord was having his own financial and marital problems (which was why I was able to purchase the property at a tax sale) and decided it was best to get rid of the nosey tenant rather than pay to fix the bug problem.

I had the entire building exterminated and never had a problem with any of the tenants there.

## DEALING WITH FORMER OWNERS

But what if you are dealing with angry, upset, and hostile former owners who feel they have been taken advantage of by the system, or who had a dispute with the former lender? My biggest advice here is that you don't want to get in the middle of it.

State laws determine statutory rights of redemption and challenges by former owners. On the rare occasion when you or your attorney feels there are substantial conflicts that could impact your *ownership*, then you might want to wait a bit before doing any substantial improvements to the property. Your investment will still be protected by the procedures of the county and tax lien laws. I have only had one instance where the county later cancelled the sale and paid me back my money (plus costs) due to a legal challenge from a former owner. If I were you, I wouldn't lose a lot of sleep worrying about this issue.

The former owner must have a valid reason to challenge the tax lien and your ownership of the property, such as that the tax sale was unfair, the sale was held before the required statutory notice period, or you or other owners were not given notice. Even then, their lawsuit action would be against the county, not against you.

The best way to avoid challenges is to do your homework and due diligence, including running a title search and making sure you know who owns the property and who has an interest in it. Have all title documents recorded and keep good records in case you need to prove ownership in court.

I know a story of an investor who purchased a tax deed at an auction. When he went to the property to talk to the owners, he found out that they had just purchased the property from the people who lost it in the tax sale. They showed him a copy of the deed and all of the paperwork they obtained from the title company. Needless to say, this created quite a bit of worry from both sides. Who really owned the property?

It turned out the title company that the current owners had used to conduct the sale was negligent and did not run a title update before they closed the sale. The property had three mortgages on it, all of which went into foreclosure, but no one caught the tax lien that was still open and active. The current owners purchased the property for $350,000 and they had a title insurance policy in place on it. However, the investor, having bought a tax lien, was in superior position on title and was the legal owner.

After several frantic phone calls, the underwriter who wrote the title insurance policy ended up contacting the investor and negotiating a settlement with him for $200,000 to buy his tax deed, which he had paid $18,000 for! The title underwriter had to buy it because it was his company's error; otherwise, they were going to have to pay their insured the $350,000 the new owners had paid to purchase the house.

Getting title insurance on your purchases can protect you in many different ways and I highly recommend it.

## OTHER LEGAL OR EQUITABLE
## INTEREST HOLDERS

There is a difference between having what is called *legal* title and *equitable* title. Equitable title means that you have the right to enjoy and use the property, while legal title means you own the property. For example, in a land contract, the seller sells the buyer the property and the buyer has the use and enjoyment of the property. Once the buyer pays the seller the balance of the purchase price for the land, the buyer now owns the legal ownership rights to the land. A beneficiary under a trust has an equitable interest. A trustee owns the legal title.

When a borrower takes out a mortgage on a property, the property is used as collateral for the loan. The owner retains legal and equitable ownership rights, and the lender has a security interest in the property until the borrower pays back the loan. If the borrower defaults, then the lender can foreclose and receive ownership rights and benefits to the property. The borrower no longer has any interest in the property after the redemption period passes, unless the borrower can prove there was wrongful foreclosure, fraud, or a mistake occurred.

State laws vary with respect to the way a judgment lien can be collected against a piece of real property. However, the process pretty much works like this. The person or entity who is awarded a judgment can obtain an Abstract of Judgment and record it in the county where the judgment debtor owns real property. A notice must be sent to the owner of the property. If and when the property is sold, the lien must be paid off with the sale proceeds or title cannot pass to the new buyer.

As a general rule, a tax sale will negate all mortgage liens, mechanic's liens, judgment liens, and other challenges that could come up. In the rare exceptions or complicated title issues, that's where a quiet title action solves everything.

# AVOIDING AND ELIMINATING RISK

*Real estate cannot be lost or stolen, nor can it be carried away. Purchased with common sense, paid for in full, and managed with reasonable care, it is about the safest investment in the world.*

—Franklin D. Roosevelt

There are risks in just about every financial decision you make in life. Heck, there's risk in just getting out of bed each day. But the best advice is to find ways to minimize, reduce, or eliminate practical risks in any way that you can. This is known as creating *Zero Risk.*

In tax lien and tax deed investing, possible risks you could encounter include market risk, liquidity risk, property risk, mortgages, IRS liens, bankruptcy, mechanic's liens, environmental risks, and unforeseen events faced when foreclosing or perfecting your title. Of course, proper research and investigation prior to making a real estate investment allows you to weed out the good investments from the bad and therefore helps to make your investment less risky.

Keeping track of your investments, and in particular the redemption periods involving your tax lien certificates, allows you to easily keep on top of deadlines and dates so that you can make intelligent and informed decisions about acquiring property and later selling and disposing of it. Educating yourself about certain myths associated with mortgages, lien priority, and environmental risks also plays a big role in how you deal with and avoid these risks. Many people will shy away or even run from properties that have an IRS lien on them. That's okay with me—it eliminates competition, since I understand the risks and know how to deal with them.

Finally, every investment we enter into should include serious thought about an exit strategy, so that when the time is right, we can cash in and move on to the next investment opportunity.

## RISK ELIMINATION

The whole basis of *Zero Risk Real Estate* is to act smartly and intelligently to eliminate as much risk as realistically possible. While there is certainly an element of risk in any real estate transaction, there is also risk in walking across the street. But as long as you look both ways and don't jump out into traffic, you'll be just fine and you've eliminated all practical risk involved. Let's take a look at the most common forms of risk that you'll encounter in a tax sale investment, and how you should react.

### Market Risk

Here we are talking about the overall economic picture. Market risk refers to the possibility that an investment portfolio will lose value due to changes

97

in typical market risk variables, such as interest rates and stock prices. While you may find property easier to sell in a good economy, there is little other effect the market can have on your investment if you plan correctly, since you are not dealing with retail real estate pricing. Unlike the above mentioned market variables, tax lien investments remain steady despite the economy. This is because the interest rates on tax liens are legally mandated and not susceptible to the fluctuations of the market, and so your rate of return is fixed or it could go up. The stock market has no effect. The bond market has no effect. The cost of living, inflation, Consumer Price Index, Dow Jones, Justin Bieber, and Donald Duck have no effect. Therefore, when it comes to the economic market, your investment is *Zero Risk*.

## Property Risk

In Chapter 2, you learned about conducting basic property research and identifying attractive lien investments. The converse is also important. You should be able to recognize warning signs that tell you a particular property is worthless and will likely end up costing you in the long run. In the context of tax liens and tax deeds, the term *worthless* is literal—having no worth or value. Finding yourself saddled with a worthless property is a risk you can and should be able to easily avoid when properly researched. Researching properties carefully is naturally a critical step, and can help you avoid the pitfalls of most or virtually all property risk. Otherwise, you could get stuck with swampland or an unbuildable lot, and all your hard work, time, and money will be lost. Here are a few issues that can be considered red flag indicators that the property you're considering could likely be an investment risk.

- *Property taxes are not in keeping with taxes on other properties in the area.* In general, taxes will be higher on valuable properties as opposed to worthless properties. Although certainly no guarantee, buying somewhat more expensive liens can help give you some measure of security that your property is likely to be worth something, even in a worst-case scenario of having to foreclose.
- *The property has been condemned or been cited for numerous violations.* Local government, or the building department specifically, should have a complete file on the history of the property as well as information on any condemnation proceedings.
- *The property is unbuildable due to size, zoning, or other impediments.* Not a problem for existing structures, but weird vacant lots—stay away from these!

- *Is the property landlocked or does it have right-of-way issues?* These will be clearly evident in the GIS maps or recorded plat maps. Again, many states have laws that protect an owner from this happening, but this could be a real bargain for an adjacent property owner.

  Not long ago, I bought a tax deed parcel that was vacant in a subdivision. My research indicated that the next-door neighbor had installed a pool. It was cheaper for him to buy the parcel from me than to relocate or demolish his pool and deck. Nobody else bothered to bid on the parcel.

  - *Structural concerns.* While these may sometimes be hard to determine and assess, you should look for evidence of cracked or unsettled foundations, walls that are not square, fire damage, or even stripping, where anything of value has been ripped out from the property for resale. I have seen property with furnaces, wiring, copper pipes, light fixtures, and even toilets that had been ripped out for resale. Most of that stuff can easily be replaced, but it cuts into your budget.

  - *Low fair market value in comparison to other properties in the area.* If the fair market value is much lower than that of other properties, you have good reason to wonder what might be wrong with the land or the improvements on the land. It might be that this was the loner house that was original to the site, and later a subdivision was built up around it. Or it could simply be another case of bulldozer bait.

  - *Contamination and other environmental issues.* This is probably one of the top concerns I hear from new investors, but it's not really a cause for alarm. There are some built-in protections you have from the nondisclosure of these types of items, but while you are doing your initial due diligence, these risks can usually be readily assessed. Check the EPA's site for known areas of contamination and environmental issues. The county may also have a page on their website that talks about any local environmental issues, or you can simply call and ask. Nondisclosure of known items is justification for the cancellation and refund of a sale. Again, with proper research and evaluation of the parcel, all of these issues can be properly mitigated. Result to you in the end? *Zero Risk.*

## Liquidity Risk

In my book, this is the only real justifiable risk in tax lien and tax deed investing. But it is certainly manageable on your end.

An investment is considered a *liquidity risk* if invested funds are tied up and can't be liquidated (that is, turned into cash flow) within a short period.

When you invest in tax lien certificates, you run a liquidity risk because your money is unavailable to you throughout the redemption period, which can take up to two, three, or even five years in some cases.

Unlike some other investments, such as CDs or bonds, with tax liens you can't withdraw your money even at a penalty. Once you make the payment on your investment, that money is out of your hands until the property owner pays back all the taxes, interest, and other associated costs. If that doesn't happen, then your money remains tied up through the deed acquisition and possible foreclosure process. Although there is a small, secondary market where you could sell your position to another investor, tax liens are not liquid investments, so plan accordingly. Always invest with money you do not need right away.

## Price

> **CHIP TIP:** In real estate, price solves everything, and every property will sell at a certain price.

Remember that you acquired the property for far less than it's worth. That means you will profit even if you have to sell the property for lower than you had initially hoped. Accept it as part of the nature of the business, take your profit, and reinvest in the next property. Even if you only break even, you will have learned a valuable lesson along the way.

Sellers who overprice their properties are sorry later because the property just sits on the market, even if they use a Realtor to market it. While overpricing is always the wrong strategy to use when selling property, it has less effect when it's a seller's market because property appreciation may catch up to a higher listing price over a certain period of time. But again, the longer a property remains on the market, the less luster and attraction it has to buyers, and many times you end up getting less than if you had priced it properly to begin with.

Here is an example of how overpricing can backfire on you. Let's say you price your property $50,000 more than current market value. What happens is that Realtors and buyers use your home to compare it to homes that are priced within market value or under, and they consider you to be a seller who is unrealistic and someone to avoid doing business with. Then you realize you must reduce your price, but it may be too late because if market conditions turn, as they have in the past few years, you may end up taking a lot less than if you had priced your property at market value and run to the bank with your money when you had the chance. You've also lost valuable time—and that, you can't get back.

Bottom line: If you have to take a bit less to get the property sold, you are still better off than if you hadn't started investing in tax liens, and you've improved your overall financial position. Understanding that every property sells at a certain price point, and knowing that the funds are protected by the government, equals *Zero Risk* for you.

## Mortgages

This one may surprise you. Although the priority of most liens is determined by date of recording, property tax liens have certain privileges. Tax liens have priority over senior liens including mortgages, regardless of when they are filed, since taxes have been a lien against property since before the dawn of time. Mortgages do not take first lien precedence over tax liens, and the lender's interests are extinguished when the tax lien property is foreclosed on.

Sorry, lenders—you lose. Again, you have *Zero Risk* because the worst-case scenario is typically one in which the lender will pay off the tax lien and you will get your money. If the lenders don't pay you off, they lose their rights to collect and you are placed into first lien position on the title.

## IRS Liens

Contrary to popular belief, you won't run into these very often. And if and when you do, they are very manageable situations.

When a property owner fails to pay personal or business income taxes, the federal government may file a lien against the property. In fact, they will usually file a lien against anything that has that person's name on it! While this federal lien takes precedence over most other liens in the event of bankruptcy, if a particular lien falls under the category of liens placed under local law for the purpose of securing property taxes, then such liens supersede the IRS lien. In short, local tax liens trump federal tax liens. But they do get a chance to redeem! When property is sold at public auction on which the IRS holds a tax lien, the US government has the right of redemption for 120 days from the date of such sale (26 USC Section 3712(g) and 7425 (d)). The IRS will pay the actual amount paid for the property by the bidder, plus interest at 6 percent per annum from the date of the sale, plus the expenses of sale that exceed any income that has been received from the property. There's your safety net. If you do find an IRS lien against a property, it is possible to get that lien released by the IRS, which will make the process quicker and easier. In some cases, the lien may have already been satisfied and not even be valid any longer. It is not the IRS's job to release the lien—it's the property owner's job. Sometimes you just need to ask for a copy of the release and take it down to be recorded in the county records. Again, the bottom line risk on IRS liens? *Zero*.

## Bankruptcy

If the property owner files for bankruptcy after you purchase your tax lien, it does not mean that you lose your money. In most cases, it just means a delay. It will simply take a longer period of time for you to see your profits because you'll have to wait for the bankruptcy process to run its course (maybe another 120 days or so). In extremely rare cases, the bankruptcy settlement could result in the court lowering the interest rate you originally held or possibly lowering the priority of your lien. I personally have never seen this happen, but I have heard of one such case from a fellow investor. The key factor here is that you act quickly upon receipt of a bankruptcy notice. Consult an attorney or other expert to file a claim with the court so you can quickly get on the way to securing your investment. A property caught up in a bankruptcy is obviously not an ideal choice, even if only because it further delays your ability to liquidate. Therefore, during the due diligence phase, seek out as much information as you can regarding the existence or potential of bankruptcy of the previous or current property owner. Bankruptcy filings are a matter of public record, so the information is readily accessible. Either way though, the property taxes will have to eventually be paid, including any and all interest and fees. So although it may take a little longer, the advantage still goes to you.

## Mechanic's Liens

Builders and contractors are protected by state laws when they perform any type of major work on a property. Installation of furnaces, air conditioners, electrical or plumbing systems, room additions, finishing off a basement— these are just a few examples of items covered under these laws.

When a property owner fails to pay a contractor, or a general contractor fails to pay a subcontractor who did work on the property, that contractor has the right to file a *mechanic's lien* on the property to ensure ultimate payment for services rendered. In most states, mechanic's liens do not survive the tax sale process since the tax lien has supreme priority. The contractors have received notice just like any other lien holder, and have had a chance to redeem their position. Also, mechanic's liens typically are only valid for one year from the date they are filed. You will still need to make sure that all lien holders were given proper notice and made aware of the sale if the lien has not expired. Otherwise, the lien holders have the right to come back and contest your purchase. But even in that case, they would have to pay you off for your tax lien position plus interest and costs.

Either way, these liens must be filed and recorded in the public record to even have a basis for a claim, so they are easily identifiable and avoidable. Once again—*Zero Risk*.

### Environmental Risk

One of the biggest fears of beginning investors is getting involved with a property that has environmental problems. This shouldn't be a worry. As I mentioned, to quickly determine whether or not a property presents an environmental liability risk, check to see if the state has an environmental website, check the EPA's site location listings, or maybe even a page or link on the county's website. Properties with known environmental problems are often listed on such sites for obvious reasons, and usually are well known to local professionals and county officials. Steer clear of any properties on this list! You may find yourself saddled with expensive cleanup and a property no one will want to buy from you. The research methods that I've shown you will generally reveal such problems. But in the unlikely event that the problems do not get revealed, and you are sold a tax deed that has an undisclosed environmental problem, you are still protected. In the same way that lenders are protected from foreclosing on a property and inheriting an environmental problem unknown to them, the same laws are in place to protect you from liability. If you find yourself in this position, check with your attorney, but this is realistically *Zero Risk*.

## THE RISKS OF ILLIQUIDITY

 Tax liens are not a liquid investment! Plan on your money being tied up for the entire term, plus six months if necessary for foreclosure.

As I stated in the beginning of this book, tax lien investing is a get-rich-slow plan. For this reason, you should be wary of investing critical funds that you may need for other purposes. Tax lien investing is certainly not something you should be engaging in with emergency resources. Instead, consider stocking a percentage of your income away, or using a qualified retirement plan with the goal of investing the saved money in tax sale ventures (see Chapter 8). Remember that, in addition to the money required to actually purchase the lien or property at sale (including back taxes and associated costs), you may be required to continue paying all subsequent taxes on the property. If you don't pay, the property will once again be listed in the next tax sale. But *you are still in a secure position*. To avoid losing your possible foreclosure profit on the investment, you should be sure you have the funds available for the interim costs until the owner redeems or you sell or assign.

You should also keep in mind that, if you foreclose on the property and attempt to resell, it's possible your money may be tied up if you're unable to sell for some time. Plan on six months, although this is dependent on market conditions and how aggressively you market the property. The point is that you may be unable to liquidate immediately. This can be a challenge but it is absolutely a manageable risk.

## MANAGING THE PROPERTY

One of the other risks you face is managing the property. If you do acquire the property by foreclosing after the tax lien redemption period expires or you purchase a tax deed, you will have to consider how you can effectively manage your property. Do you have the time or contacts to take care of initial maintenance, lawn or snow removal, or tenants?

Property management takes time, but it doesn't have to be yours. You will want to hire a team of helpers such as contractors and repair people and put together your own property management team if you start to acquire multiple properties. Use a good online software system such as Buildium (www .Buildium.com) to help you with your property management endeavors. I love their system because it's inexpensive, scalable, and web-based.

If you own multiple properties out of the area or out of state, or are an international investor, you may want to consider hiring a professional property management company to collect rents, fill vacancies, and take care of routine maintenance items. Using a good property management company can end up saving you time and money so you can concentrate on your tax lien and tax deed investment strategies and acquiring new investments.

I have one investor client who lives in Brazil. He has purchased numerous tax deed properties, established a US-based corporation, and hired a local man to manage the properties on a percentage basis. In today's global economy, there are no boundaries! He manages everything from his office in Sao Paulo and has never physically visited the properties.

Whether you decide to manage the property yourself or hire a management company, here is a basic checklist to keep in mind.

- Educate yourself about your local real estate market. Check out rental rates for competing properties.
- Conduct routine inspections on the property, and purchase maintenance plans and contracts for multiple properties whenever possible.
- Check local housing and rental requirements, screen your tenants well with credit reports and background checks, and make sure to keep the good tenants happy.
- Don't stretch your budget and take out excess equity from the property. If market values decline, you could find yourself unable to manage the downturn.
- If you do decide to use a management company, check with at least three companies to find out what services they perform and how much they charge. Their fee should be based upon a percentage of net profits to incentivize them.
- Put together your own team of property managers and contractors that you can have direct control over.

# LIQUIDATION AND CASHING IN

*Money is not the most important thing in the world. Love is. Fortunately, I love money.*

—Jackie Mason

$\mathbf{N}$ow that you've foreclosed, you're the proud owner of a property you were able to smartly acquire for *far* less than its market value. What that means is that you're sitting on a gold mine that could bring you a tremendous return. The key is to determine the most effective way to manage this deal so you're sure to get the full benefit of your investment.

But any time you consider any kind of investment, you need to evaluate several key factors. These include the cost, the risk, the return, objectives, time period, and of course—cashing in.

When I wrote the book *Cashing In on Pre-foreclosures and Short Sales* (Wiley, 2009), I spent a great deal of time talking about the need for developing an exit plan before you even start, and building a team that can help you realize those objectives quickly. This type of investing is no different, except that you are dealing directly with counties as the seller, as opposed to distressed individuals.

In this chapter, we're going to take a look at your exit plan and the choices you have for cashing in. After all, that's the fun part!

## CREATING AN EXIT PLAN

Before you can create your exit strategy, you must clearly define your real estate property investment goals and objectives. Ask yourself, do you intend to make real estate investing your primary source of income? Is real estate investing supplemental income or are you building long-term wealth for you and your family? Once you have established your objectives, only then can you consider various exit strategies that will help you realistically meet those objectives.

Your strategy may involve just purchasing tax lien certificates and hoping to earn interest on your investments when the property owner redeems the property and pays the taxes. Selecting properties that you *know* will redeem, and structuring the redemption periods in staggered intervals, will create a steady return and stream of income once it is mapped out on a calendar. This is a simple and straightforward approach to creating long-term wealth with *Zero Risk*.

Or, you may want to own property by purchasing tax deeds, or to foreclose on your tax lien certificates when the opportunity arises and build an investment portfolio by buying low, rehabbing, and selling high. Some properties you may want to rehab and lease, while others you may want to rehab and flip by selling them at a higher amount than you paid and recouping your investment quicker.

While this certainly takes more energy, expense, time, and cost, the returns can be much higher. When it comes to developing your exit plan, here are the options.

### Tax Lien:

- Redemption—The property owner pays you off with interest.
- Sale of Certificate—You can sell the certificate to another investor.
- Foreclose—You can exercise your right to gain ownership upon expiration of the redemption period.

### Tax Deed:

- Hold and Rent—Retain the property and become a landlord.
- Rapid Liquidation—Sell the property at wholesale.
- Sell on Installments—The maximum profit potential possible.

Cashing in on the tax lien side is pretty straightforward, and we have already covered the redemption options. Another way to benefit from your lien/deed investment without having to foreclose or deal with the hassles of property ownership is to assign your interest to another buyer. Not all states allow investor-to-investor assignments, so as always, check the state laws before proceeding. In states that do allow this, meeting other investors and finding ways to make mutually beneficial deals can be an effective way to realize your profits early.

For example, let's say you have a lien that's nearing the end of the redemption period. Perhaps you don't want to go through the foreclosure process and deal with ownership of the property. In that case, you may be able to assign your interest to an investor who does in fact want the property and is willing to pursue foreclosure. Your fellow investor would pay you the redemption amount of your lien, including the interest you've earned thus far, and you would assign over your lien to the other investor. Another win-win.

But be forewarned: there is a very limited market for the sale of these certificates. We have investors through the Zero Risk Resource Center, and I have seen many certificates sold on sites like eBay and Bid4Assets, but your returns will be greatly diminished. You are really selling the *right to foreclose* at that point, and it requires a particular kind of investor to take you up on it.

Let's spend more time looking at what your options are when you get your hands on the property itself.

# HOLD AND RENT STRATEGY

There is a lot to be said for simply fixing up your new property and leasing it out as a landlord. You have put in a great deal of time and effort to acquire this asset, and you have a relatively low investment compared to the long-term potential return. You can not only collect monthly payments but also enjoy the initial built-in equity and have the satisfaction of watching the value of the asset grow over time.

But becoming a landlord brings its own set of challenges. Repairs, maintenance, locating and qualifying tenants, collection of rents, and of course, the occasional eviction. If the property is local, or you have a good property manager in the area, this can be pretty profitable.

The following are some of the major concerns of being a landlord.

### Making Repairs

When it comes to being a landlord, two things in life are inevitable: death and repairs. Don't even consider a property management business unless you're sure that you can pay for repairs. Landlord and tenant laws require that you make serious repairs quickly. If you don't, you could be held liable for additional damages.

The worst thing about repairs is that they normally creep up on you suddenly and often cost a lot to get the damage fixed. For example, if your tenant calls at 11:30 PM to tell you the water heater has busted and is flooding the house, you have to immediately send an emergency repairman to shut off the water and dry out the carpet.

Since it's after hours, he'll charge you double his usual hourly rate for each of the two hours he is there. On top of that, you then have to replace the water heater. Since this is a repair that needs to happen as soon as possible, the next morning you head to Sears and buy the most reasonably priced water heater you see. Not only do you have to pay for delivery and installation, but Sears won't haul away your old, broken water heater. Luckily, your repair guy offers to remove it as long as you pay him his hourly rate and cover the dump fees.

Major problems aren't the only issues you'll have to deal with. Some tenants will call you for everything. Be prepared to spend your free time changing light bulbs, replacing air filters, weeding yards, and spraying squeaky hinges. Of course, there is a way to train your tenants to take care of the little things. But that's another book.

It's because of these events that having a person on your staff to manage the property for you becomes almost a necessity. I own several houses in the same city. I pay a handyman a flat rate of $300 a month to manage these properties for me. He will go and do the needed repairs. The only additional expenses I have are for materials, which I would have to pay for anyway. I am telling you now, having that 2 AM phone call go to him instead of me is worth every penny of the $300 I pay him.

## Collecting Rent

You'll have great tenants who pay the rent on time every month. You'll have good tenants who slip up from time to time but always let you know ahead of time when to expect the rent. And then you'll have the tenants who don't pay and don't call. As a landlord, you're going to have to pay a bill collector from time to time.

Before you start renting, ask yourself if you will be comfortable when you have to confront your tenants. Keep in mind that you'll have to make judgment calls as a landlord. For example, imagine you've had a tenant for six months, and then one month he doesn't pay the rent. You don't hear from him for a week. Finally, you decide to call, and the tenant tells you he won't be able to pay for another seven days. You'll have to make a choice, either to let the tenant slide or to start the eviction process. Make sure you will be comfortable making this kind of decision and sticking to it. My advice would be to give a normally good tenant one chance. So in this case give him the seven days he says he will need. If he then doesn't pay the rent and comes up with another story, don't lose any more time—start getting your eviction documentation together. Experience has taught me that once someone is behind, it is really difficult and unlikely for them to catch up.

## Dealing with Problem Tenants

Most of your tenants will pay the rent, treat the property like their own, and keep the neighbors happy. But at some point, you'll inevitably have a problem tenant. As a property owner, I've seen my fair share of problems. Once, I agreed to rent a property to three college students. By the second month, they stopped paying rent. I went to the house to talk to them. When the door opened, I was greeted by a large pole coming out of the ground and extending to the ceiling. The tenants had installed a fireman's pole in the house, complete with a hole in the first floor ceiling and a pile of concrete on the ground. The tenants promised to pay the rent and repair the damage from the pole. Not surprisingly, they didn't.

The third month, I filed for an eviction. After the hearing, the tenants went back to the house and removed their stuff before the sheriff and I got there. When I went inside, I found graffiti on the wall, concrete in the toilets and sink, mold in the appliances, stains on the floors, and a bright, shiny fireman's pole.

If you're going to be a landlord, you're going to have to handle tenants fighting with other tenants, tenants doing damage to your investment, and tenants who don't pay. You'll need to know the eviction laws in your state well, and be prepared to use them. Of course, not all tenants are a problem, and the bad ones are the exception—but you need to be prepared.

The absolutely best thing you can do to avoid this is to properly screen your tenants before renting to them. I learned this the hard way early on in my career. Sometimes you are just so anxious to get the property rented that you forget about common sense. Do background and credit checks on everyone before you rent to them. You don't have to pay for these yourself. I charge every prospective tenant a $50 application fee when they apply to rent one of my properties. This does two things. First, it screens out the people who aren't really serious about renting the property, since you have to be really interested to spend the $50. Second, it tells you what kind of risk you are taking when you rent to this person. Think of a rental agreement as a marriage. They are very easy to get into, and very hard and expensive to get out of!

## Surviving Evictions

Your state's landlord and tenant laws make evictions *seem* pretty simple. To start one, you go to the local court, file a notice, schedule a court date, and show up on that date. The judge then tells the tenant to leave. The tenant heads straight back to your property, quickly packs up, and walks out the door. No harm, no foul, right?

In reality, evictions are often extremely costly and time-consuming. Even if you evict your tenant successfully, you likely will have incurred major expenses and lost significant time in the process.

I've been through it before. Here's an example scenario of how an eviction can work out:

- The tenant doesn't pay his rent on the first.
- The fifth rolls around and the tenant still hasn't paid, but you decide to wait five more days and try to avoid filing an eviction.
- The tenth comes and you still haven't heard from the tenant. You go to the court, pay your fee (which ranges from $35 to $100 or more, depending on your state), and the court clerk tells you that the judge is backed up. They can't schedule your hearing until next month.

Once the court date rolls around, you're out two months' rent. The judge decides in your favor, but now you have to schedule a time with the sheriff to complete the eviction. That takes another five days.

You show up with the sheriff after the five days and find that the tenant has departed and left piles of stuff behind. According to the law in many states, you now have to rent a storage locker to hold the tenant's belongings. That costs you another $50. Now, if you were very lucky, you have a vacant apartment that needs cleaning and re-renting. Even at your luckiest, you'll probably lose at least one month's more rent while you look for a tenant. If you weren't so lucky, the tenant caused some damages, which you will have to repair before you can rent the apartment again.

In the end, the breakdown looks something like this:

- Four months' lost rent at $750: $3,000
- Cost to file in court: $35
- Cost to rent storage: $50
- Cost to make repairs: $500
- *Total cost to evict the tenant*: $3,585

Ouch! These eviction costs are another reason why it pays to take extra time to investigate a potential tenant before you sign the lease documents. It's obviously cheaper to leave the place empty for a few months while you are finding the right tenant than spending the time and money to evict them.

## Keeping Your Property Safe

If a tenant is injured on a property that you own, there is a good chance you'll be sued. Sure, you have homeowners liability insurance, but you always have the duty to keep your property properly maintained and in good working order so as to avoid contributing to potential mishaps. By keeping your units safe, no matter what it takes, you greatly decrease your chance of trouble in this area.

In order to prevent problems, you'll need to know the building and safety codes in your area and follow them by attending to regular maintenance and checking on your properties periodically. It may take a lot of work, but can save you a costly legal battle later on.

That's another reason why I try to have a handyman on my staff. He will go and collect the rent every month and look around the property to see if any potential hazards are forming.

**Paying Taxes**

One thing you can't overlook is taxes. Renting property is your business, and so you'll have to report what you have earned when you file your income taxes every year. But one tax commonly overlooked is the property tax. If you own the home you live in plus one rental house, your property tax bill could be double what you were paying before you purchased the rental. This is because, in most jurisdictions, rental properties are taxed at a higher rate than principal residences. Make sure you understand the effect taxes will have on your bottom line and that you are prepared to pay them.

There are some ways in which taxes can work to a property owner's advantage, particularly in a down housing market. Consider, for example, that you need to sell your home but can't recoup what you paid for it. If you sell it as your primary home, you can't claim the loss on your taxes. However, if you turn it into a rental property first, you may be able to claim the loss as a business loss against any rental income received or against your ordinary income. This can decrease your tax bill by thousands of dollars, especially if you claim a large loss and have a high income.

Investing in rental properties is a great way to make money. Just remember that being a landlord is not all fun and games. You'll work hard for your money and may be faced with adversity from time to time. Buying rental property is not for everyone. It should be an investment option you consider only after you've achieved a certain level of financial independence.

If your new investment can be considered a vacation property or is located in an area that you would love to visit periodically, then you may want to keep it as a second home or cottage. To cover your initial investment and expenses, you could even sell off a percentage of ownership, creating what is known as a *fractional ownership* by friends, associates, or family members. This is quite common in higher value and vacation areas like Hawaii, Washington, DC, or Florida. I have a friend who makes an incredible living dealing in nothing more than fractional ownership properties in Lake Tahoe, Nevada.

Another way to turn a profit on a property in a vacation area is to rent it out seasonally. Instead of doing fractional ownership or a time share, you keep 100 percent ownership of the property and rent it out during the season. These are the months most people want to visit the area and they vary from state to state.

One of my students has a property in Florida that was picked up as a tax lien. The owner failed to redeem, and possession was taken through a tax deed. It was for a condominium unit in a very nice building overlooking the intercoastal waterway. Even with the depressed real estate market in Florida, he could have very easily flipped this property and made a nice profit. It only needed some minor work inside, and the kitchen was outdated and had to be upgraded. It was a two bedroom, 1.5 bath condo with a deck/patio overlooking the water—your typical little slice-of-heaven location.

But he ran into a problem that many of you can expect to happen at some point in your career. Your spouse or significant other may decide they want to keep the property. For him, it was his wife. All he heard was, "It's the perfect getaway for us, can't we keep it?" So he found a way to compromise. In Florida, the seasonal months when everyone wants to vacation there are mostly December through April. So what he did was to upgrade the kitchen and furnish the place nicely, but inexpensively, with furniture that was designed to last and be easy to clean and maintain. He spent a grand total of $8,000 on the whole project.

He then placed the property for rent seasonally with a local Realtor. They were able to find tenants to rent this place for six months of the year at $2,000 a month. This gave him a $12,000 yearly income from the property. The carrying costs for an entire year, including HOA fees and utilities, come to around $2,000, so he has a $10,000 net profit, and more importantly, his wife has another place to vacation for six months out of the year while the unit is being rented. Talk about a win-win!!

## Rapid Liquidation

The most common approach used by tax deed investors to cash in on the investment is simply selling at a wholesale price. While you could certainly list the property with a professional Realtor and try to get a retail sale, the time versus return equation might make that choice expensive. The holding costs, combined with tying up funds that could be used for other tax sale transactions, make a rapid liquidation the better play. Still, use a local Realtor to help you out—it's worth it. But drastically discount the price to allow someone else to also make a little profit. It'll go faster, and you'll sleep better! Having $100 in your hands right now to reinvest is almost always going to be better than waiting three months and maybe getting $200 then.

---

**CHIP TIP:** Look for speed in selling—not maximizing profits!

---

Since you've acquired the property for so little, it would be highly unlikely that you would see a loss on a sale, but time is worth money, especially when it's yours and it's getting eaten up with marketing time and holding costs. Instead, think about pricing your property way below the market for a quick sale—it's the smart thing to do.

Remember, price solves all problems. A piece of property will always sell at some price when exposed to a market, and at this point, you just want to move on to the next deal as quickly as possible.

You could even offer to let the previous owner buy back the property. A move like that would be a three-way win: the owner finds a way out of a tough situation, the government gets the taxes it needs, and you've done a good deed while still getting a decent return on your investment.

Unless you're dying to be a property owner, selling low and flipping within a short time frame brings you a quick profit and puts you in a position to do more investing, which potentially increases your long-term return.

This is also known as *turning over your inventory*. I know many investors who try to keep a 20- to 30-property rolling inventory going at any given time. They don't hold any property for more than a few months, and for every property they sell, they invest in a new one.

## CREATING LONG-TERM WEALTH USING INSTALLMENTS

Another solution is to combine these two approaches. This is by far my favorite technique, and one that will propel you like a rocket on your road to creating wealth. I have generated incredible returns using this strategy, and I've sold property to investors all over the world this way.

You see, I don't like being a landlord, but I love the monthly income. By selling the property on an installment plan, you can do both. Experienced real estate investors will tell you that the real value is not necessarily in the price, but rather in the *terms* associated with the deal. This is true on the selling side as well as the buying side.

For example, if you had $100,000 to invest in a property, would you rather pay $100,000 in cash at time of closing, or $10,000 down and the balance of $90,000 over the next 10 years at 7 percent interest? Assuming the property is generating some cash flow, then the obvious choice is buying it on terms. But here's the real question: is the property worth more because of the terms? The answer is clearly yes.

The inverse principle is what says there is a discount for paying cash. When you pay 100 percent cash for something like real estate, you expect to get a discount, right? Let's show you how to make this work for you when you sell your property. Here is a real-life example of a deal I just completed.

### Property: 3-unit multi-family house with detached garage

| | |
|---|---|
| Tax deed purchase: | $4,000 |
| Legal fees: | $850 |
| Eviction fees: | $200 |
| Cleanup crew: | $1,250 |
| Total acquisition cost: | $6,300 |
| Assessed value: | $84,000 |
| Value fixed up: | $118,000 |
| Repairs needed: | $28,000 |

This property was in decent shape, but had gone through a foreclosure about 18 months prior to the tax sale. The bank walked away from the property. There was still a tenant in one of the units who had been living rent-free with no landlord for over a year. Two of the units were uninhabitable due to necessary repairs, appliances, and so on. Area rental rates indicated that the units would rent for a combined total of $1,500 per month.

I could have invested money in repairing the property, and a local appraiser indicated that the value when fixed up and rented would be about $118,000. I elected a different route. I advertised in several sites such as Craigslist, FreeClassifieds.com, ClassifiedAds.com, and others; all of the ads directed the readers to an eBay auction.

Now, this is critically important: the eBay auction I set up offered the property at a 50 percent wholesale discount, and the auction bid was not for the total price, but for *only the down payment!* The winning bidder got the property for $42,000 (50 percent of assessed value), on a 5-year note at 9 percent interest; on a 30-year amortization, the payment was $337.94 per month. The winning bid was received from an investor in South America for $2,550. Now let's take a look at my return.

### Zero Risk Liquidation Results:

| | |
|---|---|
| Down payment received: | $ 2,550 |
| Principal amount financed: | $42,000 |
| Interest received (60 months): | <u>$18,546</u> |
| *Total received:* | $63,096 |
| Less initial investment: | $ 6,300 |
| *Total profit:* | $56,796 |

That is a profit of over 900 percent or 180 percent per year! The best part is, I recoup my initial investment in just over a year; I don't have to fix up the property; I don't have to be a landlord; and I don't have to worry about the collateral—the purchaser is increasing the value. All I have to do is collect the payments, and even that is automated.

Think about this whole scenario for a moment. Let it really sink in, and understand how powerful the concept of selling on terms was. The property would have been far less attractive if I had wanted $42,000 in cash up front, and it would have been much tougher to sell. The investor would have still gotten a pretty good deal, but would have had to lay out more cash for the repairs, and it would have limited my market.

I let him save his cash. He will enjoy a great cash flow on the property when it's rented out, and he bought it at a wholesale price to boot. And I don't have to worry about not getting paid, or I can simply foreclose and sell it again—on terms.

## Rinse and Repeat

With vacant land parcels, you can do the same thing and sell to a new homebuyer or builder on terms with a zero down payment. Since the cost for these parcels to you is minimal, you are trying to create the long-term cash flow. After you structure one of these transactions, simply "rinse and repeat," as they say.

Once you have set up several of these types of deals, you will be experiencing a monthly cash flow that many people only dream about. You'll do it without the hassle of property management and landlord responsibilities, and you'll do it all—*Zero Risk!*

# ADVANCED STRATEGIES

*I like thinking big. If you're going to be thinking anything, you might as well think big.*

—Donald Trump

# 8

# ADVANCED STRATEGIES

Now that you understand the basics of tax lien and tax deed investing, and the principal strategies of generating profits, let's take some time to look at some other more sophisticated strategies you can start to explore. Once you've gotten your feet wet, you're going to want to expand your activities and look for other creative ways to generate profits. These might include ways of obtaining investment capital, corporate investing, retirement investing and tax strategies, as well as investing in unique property types such as cell towers, billboards, access roads, community parks, and easements. Let's start with some financing strategies.

## USING TRADITIONAL FUNDING

Your new tax property acquisitions have value, and sometimes they have great value. You've put in the research, followed the process, and invested time and money. One strategy is to then leverage out your property using traditional funding sources.

Traditional funding is recommended if you are planning on holding onto your real estate properties over a long period of time, say five years or more. While the rules have certainly changed on the types of terms you can get when using traditional financing from banks and other financial institutions, you still might want to jump through the hoops when you want to get your initial investment dollars back out.

Traditional financing means you must meet the lender's guidelines, which are much stricter than obtaining money from private money or hard money lenders. Financial institutions must follow federal and state lending laws, provide disclosures, and do not have the flexibility that private lenders have in making lending decisions. These lenders are more interested in your creditworthiness and your debt-to-income ratio when they are considering lending you money, as well as in the current market value of the property.

Since the property serves as collateral for the loan, if you default, they want to know that they can recoup most or all of their money from foreclosing on the property or going after your other assets for any deficiencies. Of course, there is no way for anyone to predict whether property values will appreciate or depreciate and lose value, but you need to understand that lenders are interested in making loans with the least amount of risk possible.

But you have one advantage—equity. Even if you can get only a 40 percent LTV (loan to value) loan, that will typically make it a cash-free investment for you.

Let's use a practical example:

Say you purchased a tax deed for a piece of property that is worth $180,000. The cost of the tax deed was $20,000. Now you want to use your equity in that property to go out and buy more tax deeds. Using traditional financing methods, even with shaky credit, you could get a very low LTV loan on this property for perhaps 40 percent of its fair market value.

So 40 percent of its value of $180,000 would give you a loan amount of $72,000 at an interest rate of around 5.0 percent, using current figures. If you took out a 5-year balloon loan that was amortized over 30 years, then your monthly payments would only be $386.51 per month. (A 5-year balloon note means you make payments for 5 years at the same rate you would if you were paying off the loan in 30 years, except that after 5 years, your last payment would be a *balloon* payment for whatever the balance remaining on the loan is at that time.)

You have now leveraged your investment to generate $72,000 cash for you at a cost of $386.51 a month. Now, if you are renting that property for perhaps $900 a month, you still have a net profit coming in of $513.49 a month, plus you have $72,000 cash in your hand to use to invest in other tax deeds.

Even at higher interest rates and tighter qualification standards, it's not hard to see that this is a worthwhile strategy for cashing out your investment.

## TAPPING INTO PRIVATE MONEY

If traditional financing isn't available for a variety of reasons, then private money may be the solution. Sometimes referred to as *hard money loans*, these types of financing arrangements usually carry higher interest rates, higher costs, and tighter LTV ratios, but they look more carefully at the value of the property than traditional conventional bank loans do.

Private investors can be individuals, groups of people, or investment firms simply looking for a good solid rate of return. They want to recoup their investment quickly, and they're more interested in the property's value than in your credit rating. Private money lenders do not have any guidelines or rules to follow, and they do have the flexibility of lending money to whomever they want. When you work with a private money lender, you get your money right away instead of having to wait 30 to 90 days to close on a traditional loan.

At a 30 percent loan to value rate, and looking at the example we just used, a 10 percent interest rate would still be a good deal for you as well as them. Using these numbers, you would borrow $54,000 at 10 percent interest on normally a 1-year balloon note for private money. Your monthly loan payment would be $473.89. Again, if you are renting the property out for $900 a month, you have a net profit of $426.11, plus you have put $54,000 of cash buying power into your hands. The only thing to be aware of is that the balance of the loan is going to come due in 12 months. At that time you can either take out another loan and refinance the property again, or you can sell the property and cash out completely.

This type of financing is ideal when you have someone who wants to lease option a property from you for 12 months. Let's use a similar example.

You agree to a lease option contract with a purchaser who is going to buy the home in 12 months for $185,000. They are willing to pay a slight premium on the price of the house because the lease option creates a benefit to them when it comes time for them to get their permanent financing on the property. They give you a $5,000 nonrefundable deposit on the property and agree to pay you $1,200 a month in rent, with $300 of that going towards their purchase price.

You make the deal and have $5,000 in your hand and $1,200 a month income coming in. You get hard money for $54,000, as we discussed above, at 10 percent, and now your net monthly income on the property is $726.11. In 12 months both their option to purchase and your balloon payment come due. Here's what happens:

You sell the house for $185,000. You give your purchasers credit for the $5,000 they put down, plus $300 a month for 12 months ($3,600), for a total credit of $8,600. So the balance that will be paid to you for the property is $176,400.

You pay back your hard money lender what is owed on the note after 12 payments, which comes to $53,699.83. Now you have made $122,700.17 from the sale, plus $8,713.32 in rent over the 12 months ($726.11 times 12) for a total return of $131,413.49 on your original $20,000 investment. And you still were able to take out $54,000 to use during those 12 months for other investments. Talk about free money!

When it's basically free money, and you use it either to lease out the property or develop a short-term hold-and-sell to maximize your upside potential, there is completely zero risk in using this tactic. Just make sure that you can cover the payments through cash flow or by building in a reserve from the loan proceeds while you execute your exit plan.

## CORPORATE INVESTING

As you start to pursue this more, you will want to provide some additional security for yourself and your family. When you purchase a tax lien or tax deed, you are typically doing so in your own name. That means you can be held personally liable in the event of any issues with the property. While these situations are very rare, they might include any injuries that occur on the property, existing liens, environmental issues, and other concerns.

You may be able to avoid bearing personal responsibility for what goes wrong by forming a corporation or similar legal entity such as an LLC (Limited Liability Company). This cannot be simply in name only. The corporation must have a separate bank account, hold regular meetings, keep accurate records, and conduct business separate from the personal dealings of shareholders and/or owners. Failure to adhere to these rules could result in the court doing what's called *piercing the corporate veil*, which means the corporation is seen as nothing more than a transparent attempt to shield yourself, and the law will therefore bypass that corporate veil and hold you personally liable.

This can be a bit complex to navigate, and it is best to consult an attorney or other expert to manage the process for you. It's important that this formation be handled carefully, so that you don't leave yourself vulnerable to liability.

Some states have stricter requirements for setting up an LLC. In these situations you can use a subchapter S corporation as opposed to a subchapter C corporation. S corporations were set up by the IRS to allow small business owners to incorporate and obtain all of the protections of a corporation without having to bear the financial hurdles and obligations required to setup an LLC or C corporation. I personally own many S corporations and LLCs, and they are perfect vehicles for setting up small companies to manage your properties. You still need to follow the guidelines for a corporation, such as having a corporate bank account and keeping corporate and personal funds separate, but many of the other requirements are more relaxed. You should definitely consult with a tax attorney or CPA to determine what is the best vehicle for you.

While it can take a little bit of effort to set it up, if you plan on doing major investing, or teaming up with partners, then this is definitely the way to go. You can set up separate LLCs for each partnership or even each property (although I would only do it for tax deed acquisitions, not necessarily for tax liens). I have many such entities set up for my investments and for the investment partners that I work with. As a result, I never take a tax lien or tax deed in my personal name.

## LOCATING INVESTMENT CAPITAL

One of the most common questions I hear is, "Where can I find the cash to increase my investments?" Now that you understand the power of tax lien investing, the only thing holding you back is cash.

When you invest in tax liens, unlike a regular home purchase, you don't have the luxury of first finding a home and then seeking financing. Tax sales generally require that you have the funding you need immediately, and in fact, they almost always require a full cash payment on the day of purchase.

But most people don't have significant capital immediately handy, and as a result they don't take advantage of the huge investment opportunities that tax sales represent. But there is a solution: partner with other investors.

If you know someone who has ready cash, but perhaps doesn't have the time or know-how to get involved in tax lien investing, make them an offer they can't refuse. You put up the work, you put up your expertise, and they put up the cash. Agree to then split the proceeds in whatever way you both deem equitable. A private money partner can be a family member, personal friend, or even a stranger.

Alternatively, you could do what's often called *bird-dogging*—collect a finder's fee by identifying worthwhile properties for other investors so you're not actually buying the property yourself. You simply get paid for hunting down the deals, then representing the true investor's interest at the auction. It's the perfect symbiotic relationship.

An investor friend of mine makes quite a good living off of bird-dogging. In fact, you could say he went from rags to riches in a very short time. He enjoyed the sport of hunting down sellers and finding great deals on properties. Since he didn't have the cash to purchase the deed himself, he would relay the information to another friend who paid him a finder's fee. Now my friend uses bird-dogs who find him deals while he sits back and accumulates his real estate portfolio of super cheap investment properties.

I also use bird-dogs at times, since students bring me deals from around the country, and we partner on the eventual split of the proceeds. This way, I can be in many places at the same time, and my bird-dog partner acts as my local eyes, ears, and feet on the ground.

While bird-dogging is a fairly common approach, just be aware that some property tax auctions require ID, and also require that you purchase the tax liens in your name or a company name. Some auctions also limit the number of parcels that you can buy within a given lot so that other investors have equal access. This prevents a representative of a large conglomerate from monopolizing the auction.

## INVESTING USING RETIREMENT ACCOUNTS

Looking for a way to invest tax-deferred, or even tax-free? Well then, this strategy will really get your attention.

If you want to invest for your retirement, you may be able to invest with before-tax funds in a Self-Directed Individual Retirement Account (SDIRA). Regular IRAs are typically limited to only certain investments, such as CDs and mutual funds. The SDIRA, however, allows you to make investment decisions and choose the assets you want to have placed in your portfolio. This means that you can invest in nontraditional investments like real estate. IRS regulations do require that a trustee or qualified custodian holds the IRA assets on your behalf, so be sure that the custodian you select does in fact allow real estate investments.

Such accounts are also referred to as a *Qualified Retirement Plan* or QRP. There are only certain companies around the country that allow you to set one of these up for yourself—where *you* have total control. You see, while the large firms certainly manage and maintain retirement accounts, they make their money only through commissions and fees.

There are no commissions or fees when you buy tax lien or deed investments! Since there is no incentive for the large firms to research, market, or sell these to you, very few of them offer that option.

But there are many companies that will allow you to set up an account and control your own investments. Will they charge you a fee? Of course! But it will be a nominal fee, and you can control and manage your tax lien (or even property purchases) directly from within the account, allowing it to build profits for you tax-deferred or even tax-free.

Many of these accounts even offer you the option of using a debit card, so you can fund your transactions immediately on the spot.

When investing in real estate in your IRA, technically you aren't the one buying the property—it's your IRA that is buying the property. In other words, your account owns the property and you own the account. This is an important point, especially when you're ready to complete agreements and documents, since you'll need to list your IRA as the owner.

The term self-directed IRA isn't a technical term; it merely means that your IRA is directed by you instead of by someone else. You may get conflicting answers through various institutions that say they offer self-directed IRAs, yet they restrict you from investing your IRA in the way you want. A *Truly Self-Directed IRA* (TSD IRA) is the term used to say there are no in-house custodial restrictions, and you have ultimate flexibility and control without unnecessary restrictions imposed by your IRA custodian or trustee. It basically means you don't have to check with the custodian of your IRA to see if they will allow you to make an unorthodox investment with your IRA funds. You have complete control. If you want to buy snow to sell to Eskimos, it's your call.

One of the country's top experts at setting up these types of accounts is Josh Moore with TSD-IRA (www.irallc123.com). He has set up thousands of these SDIRAs, and he has appeared as a featured guest on my radio show.

There are numerous benefits to setting up an SDIRA, including that you can turn it into an LLC and gain the benefits of both tax-deferred income and liability protection. A self-directed IRA LLC is a modern hybrid between an Individual Retirement Account and a Limited Liability Company. The combination between these two types of legal entities will give investors ironclad asset protection, tax-free growth on investments, and freedom to make and maintain investment decisions and directions at will. Although you can use a TSD IRA for various investments, if you want real estate in your IRA portfolio, the TSD IRA structure is an invaluable tool.

With a TSD IRA you will have the flexibility to move in and out of real estate deals before your competition can even make an offer. Remember, you are the boss, you have the final say. With a TSD IRA you have true checkbook control. Checkbook control means that you don't have to get approval for your investments. You make the decisions, you sign the contract, and you write the check. While your competitors who use regular IRAs to purchase real estate are on the phone trying to either get their custodians to answer their calls or explain the nature of the deal to them, you have already bid on the property, won the auction, and paid for your deal!

Most real estate IRA custodians will charge you fees based on what they are doing. This means every time they take a phone call, write a check, deposit a check, and send out a report, they are charging you a fee. With a TSD IRA you are making one investment and holding one asset; this can get the fees down to the bare minimum (usually $100 to $200 a year).

And there are some significant tax benefits to purchasing property through your TSD IRA as well. For those who make a lot of money in their investment portfolio, it has the best advantage. The earnings are tax-free at distribution compared to a traditional IRA, where the distribution is taxed. So for example, if you take a small amount, say $10,000, and parlay that into a half-million or a million dollars, in a traditional IRA you'd have to pay taxes on a million dollars, whereas using your TSD IRA saves you tremendously.

Even better, if your SDIRA or TSD IRA doesn't have enough money to pay for the entire purchase, you can finance or leverage any income-producing property to cover the difference. The property is the collateral for the loan. Since the property is an asset of the retirement plan, repayment of the underlying debt must come from contributions to or income from the property or other assets in the retirement plan. This type of loan is generally referred to as a *nonrecourse loan* because the IRA holder cannot extend credit to an IRA. In essence, you are using your IRA to buy the property and at the same time using the property as collateral to pay back your IRA for any additional monies the property may cost you. It really does seem too good to be true. You get to be your own lender!

Talk to a knowledgeable financial specialist regarding your own situation, or tap into some of our coaching calls, where we periodically interview specialists on this strategy.

## TAX STRATEGIES

While each situation is different, and we cannot provide you with personal legal or accounting advice, there are many strategies you can deploy to limit any tax liability on tax lien investments.

Forming a business entity prior to investing is often an effective way to shield yourself and your assets, and to ensure that tax laws work to your benefit or at least have minimal negative impact. Entities such as an S corporation or a properly structured Limited Liability Company can help provide significant tax benefits. You should consult your own accountant or attorney to help you determine the most effective formation for your needs.

We discussed S corporations earlier, but along with giving you the liability protection you want from a corporation, they also have significant tax benefits, the biggest of which is the *pass through tax*. What this means is that, unlike most corporate structures that get taxed at both the corporate level and then again at the personal level for each shareholder, an S corporation gets taxed only at the personal level. The corporate tax is skipped or passed through to the individual shareholders. Any time you can get taxed on income once instead of twice is a good day to be an American!

Among other issues, exploring business formation can help you avoid pitfalls related to whether your real estate investment is considered a capital gain or ordinary income (which often depends on the nature of the investment, the volume of real estate activity, and the sweat equity you put into it).

This is mostly determined by whether you are an active or passive member of the partnership or corporation. A passive member would be someone who loans the company money and just collects his share of the profits and does very little else. An active member would be someone who runs the day-to-day operations, pays the bills, manages the properties, deals with the staff, does background checks on the tenants, collects the rents, and so on. These two investors have different standings, tax-wise, within the partnership or corporation.

Either way, you will still only be liable for any taxes on the actual *gains* you realize from your investment—not on the entire amount of the investment itself. An example of a popular tax strategy that many investors use to delay paying capital gains tax is the 1031 tax exchange. With a 1031 tax exchange, you are selling an existing property and exchanging it for a like property. When you go to sell your replacement property, you pay capital gain taxes at that time, unless of course you do another 1031 exchange and buy another property. There are very strict rules as to what properties can be considered for a 1031 exchange and to what amount. If you are going to use this to delay payments of capital gains, you must speak with someone who knows this process inside and out or find yourself on the wrong end of a tax bill.

Always remember to deduct any expenses and fees you incur for each transaction, and keep accurate and detailed records.

## UNIQUE TYPES OF PROPERTY DEALS

Another type of advanced strategy involves bidding on tax lien or deed items that most people won't understand. There are many other types of parcels that get auctioned off, and as long as you have a solid exit plan in hand, then these can be very profitable. These properties could include cell towers, billboards, access roads, community parks, and other types of easements.

I recently won an auction on a fully operating cell phone tower and a full-size billboard. While they eventually got redeemed, the return was guaranteed. I have also acquired neighborhood parks, complete with basketball courts, that the community association forgot about.

Most people would say, "Why would you want to buy a tax lien on a cell tower? What are you going to do, start your own cell phone company if they don't redeem?" Actually, while that does sound like a challenge, I am purchasing the tax lien on the tower knowing that the cell phone company will definitely redeem it. The tower is worth hundreds of thousands of dollars in technology. Plus, they need it to continue to provide service to their clients. I know beyond a shadow of a doubt they are going to redeem the certificate and I am going to make my money. I just diary the redemption date in my system and wait for my profits to show up. Worst case, I would get the opportunity to sell it back to them.

These types of parcels can always be sold back to the previous owner or to a competitor if they don't get redeemed, but it's rare the transaction goes that far. Condo clubhouses, gun clubs, youth clubs, or community pools— I've seen them all be thrown up for auction. Just recently I flipped a tax deed from a River Duck Hunting Club for a quick $8,800 profit.

Another tactic that experienced investors can use is actually investing on small parcels that are *out lots* or what are referred to as *postage stamp* lots. The idea here is that the small parcel is adjacent to a larger, more valuable piece that needs the small lot, or it can be used for billboard or another type of advertising. Timeshares or fractional ownership properties are another possible tax sale investment, but you really need to understand these special scenarios.

One of my favorite finds at a tax sale is a property that is surrounded by parcels that have been bought up by a development company. I just know I have a built-in purchaser for this parcel. I mean, the last thing these developers want is to spend tens of millions of dollars building this gorgeous development of single family homes with pools and community parks and a clubhouse, and have my lot with a single-wide trailer sitting right there in the middle of their development. Yes, they will pay me a premium for my lot!

In another case, I purchased an awkward piece of land that was narrow and winding through the backyards of a couple of properties in a subdivision. Upon doing my research, I learned that the property was a bicycle path that connected two different parts of the neighborhood. The neighborhood association had forgotten to pay the taxes on this, and I was able to negotiate a deal rather quickly to sell it back to them for double what I paid. Some of those Board members were probably voted out.

Another fun strategy is to select tax liens in an area that you would like to visit or where you would like to vacation. It is always fun to attend tax lien sales in Florida during the winter months, and the activity (if properly structured) can be seen as a business trip and subject to a tax write-off. Again, you need to discuss this with your accountant—and remember, keep detailed records!

Not long ago, I traveled to the US Virgin Islands, and while I was there, took time to meet with the tax assessor to investigate their tax sale system. Mixing a little business with pleasure can be quite profitable, as well as relaxing! Hee hee—now where did I put that suntan lotion?

# TRACKING YOUR
# INVESTMENTS

*Formal education will make you a living; self-education will make you a fortune.*

—Jim Rohn

**D**on't miss a date. I can tell you from experience that with so much information coming in on auctions, lists, property research, and notices, it is easy to misplace something, or worse yet, miss a crucial filing or auction date.

Every business model comes with a golden rule. In real estate we know the mantra of location, location, location dominates. If there is anything I cannot emphasize strongly enough for tax lien and tax deed investing, it is tracking, tracking, tracking. It could very well mean the success or failure of everything you set out to accomplish by using this *Zero Risk* system, because *no* system can overcome human error.

Even if you decide to use a basic manila folder filing system and a wall calendar, it's important to establish a workable system for tracking your portfolio to avoid the risk of missing important deadlines, notification requirements, redemption dates, and other actions that could have an impact on your return. In fact, you should establish a system even before you start compiling your tax lists so you can keep track of all available properties. You don't want to miss out on a great deal just because you misplaced the information.

There is an old carpenter's saying that goes "measure twice, cut once." The idea is that once you have made the cut, you can't go back and redo it, so make sure you have your figures right before you act. The same is true for tax lien and tax deed investing. Once you have purchased a tax lien, you almost always can't undo the sale without consequences. So have your system in place first and all your information organized before you go to your first auction.

## SETTING UP A SIMPLE SYSTEM

Your system for tracking your investments doesn't have to be complex, or expensive—just workable. The important thing is that you keep *detailed* records of investments and remain diligent about recording and tracking data as you proceed, not only for investment reasons, but also for tax reasons, and to just plain keep your sanity!

This could mean using various software programs designed especially for tracking tax sale investments, or it could mean taking advantage of basic tools such as Microsoft Word and Excel. For example:

1. Use a worksheet in Excel to maintain all the contact information you may need for the various tax authorities in each of the states in which you're investing.
2. When you obtain tax sale lists, itemize the data into an Excel sheet so you can compare and contrast similar data for all properties at a glance. Some counties actually provide this in a downloadable format, which makes it really easy to track. This could include lists of the properties coming up for auction, parcel IDs, addresses, current values, types of properties, and so on. Having all this information in one place makes it much easier to pick out which properties interest you and you might want to do more research on, and which ones are just junkers.
3. Create due diligence checklist sheets that you can print out and take with you when you investigate properties. Once filled, import that data into the Excel sheet so all property information is in one place. This list should include everything you want to know about the property, so you don't waste time and have to make multiple trips to see it. You don't want to be halfway home and ask yourself, "So I forget, was there a fenced yard there or not?" Write down every conceivable thing you would need to determine a value for the property and keep it with you.
4. Track all deadlines so you don't miss an opportunity to maximize your profits. Note the date you bought your lien, when all subsequent payments are due, track the redemption period, when you need to send out 30-day notices, and so on. This is critical if you need to evict tenants or foreclose on a property. You really should be sending all of these notices out using certified mail with return receipt requested and then keeping these physical receipts in your property files. If you can't prove what date you sent a notice to an owner or tenant, then the court is going to make you start the process all over again, costing you valuable time.

An example of my basic tracking is in Figure 9.1. This system allows me to easily track the expenses of the sale plus additional costs.

Whether you buy a tracking program or go with simple office management tools, the key is to refine a system that allows you to streamline your tracking so you're able to manage multiple properties over long periods of time.

# Figure 9.1
## Tax Sale–Lien/Deed Tracking Worksheet

Property Address: _____

| DATE | TIME | ACTION | ACTUAL COST | PREMIUM COSTS | OTHER COSTS | TOTAL COST |
|------|------|--------|-------------|---------------|-------------|------------|
|      |      |        |             |               |             |            |
|      |      |        |             |               |             |            |
|      |      |        |             |               |             |            |
|      |      |        |             |               |             |            |
|      |      |        |             |               |             |            |
|      |      |        |             |               |             |            |
|      |      |        |             |               |             |            |
|      |      |        |             |               |             |            |
|      |      |        |             |               |             |            |
|      |      |        |             |               |             |            |
|      |      |        |             |               |             |            |
|      |      |        |             |               |             |            |

Note: This form can be downloaded electronically at www.ZeroRiskRealEstate.com/Bonus.

One of the most flexible and free resources to use to keep track of all of this information is Google Docs. The Internet giant offers a suite of web-based productivity applications under that name. While these applications aren't as complex or comprehensive as the leading desktop counterparts, they have other advantages over traditional software.

The most obvious of these advantages is that the applications aren't tied to a specific computer. There's no need to download and install software on a particular machine. Any computer connected to the Internet can access Google Docs. Because each user saves information to the cloud system, he or she can access the same file from anywhere. Users don't have to worry about which version of a document is the most current—it will always be saved in the Google cloud.

This solution works great when you are dealing with multiple partners across the country or the world. Multiple users can make edits to the same files at the same time. This is called *online collaboration*. Because Google Docs preserves earlier versions of documents, there's no reason to worry about irrevocably changing a file.

None of the applications within the Google Docs suite are as robust or versatile as the leading desktop productivity software packages. But Google updates the suite often, adding new features and capabilities. While the applications don't have all the bells and whistles of other software packages, they do meet basic user needs. And while Google Docs might not do everything other products can do, it does have several features that set it apart from the rest of the pack, and above all else, did I mention it's *free*!

In the Zero Risk Resource Center, we have provided you with forms, letters, and downloads in Microsoft Word and Microsoft Excel formats since these are the most commonly used. They can easily be converted into other formats, or the spreadsheet data exported and then imported into hundreds of other programs. You can also convert them into the format Google Docs uses.

## ACCRUALS AND YIELD INFORMATION

As an investor, you will want to track critical information such as investment returns, yields, and of course, expenses and profits. You will also want to track accruals and tax basis numbers for tax reporting.

The tax basis of property is generally the property's cost and holding period. Cost is the amount paid for the property in cash or other property. Where an asset is acquired in a purchase of just the asset, tax basis includes cash paid plus liabilities assumed.

For example, if you acquire a building for $10,000 cash through a tax deed and then take out a mortgage on it for $80,000, your tax basis in the building is $90,000. If multiple items of property are acquired together in a single transaction, the tax basis must generally be allocated to the items in proportion to their values at the time of acquisition.

When you set up your software tracking system, you can input your accrual basis, the face value of your premium, accrual type of interest (simple, compound, and so on) and yields, so that at any given time you can generate a report. There are special tax lien software systems that you can invest in as well.

## MAINTAINING CONTACTS AND LIEN LISTS

Your software tracking system will allow you to easily update contact information and lien lists so that you can track all your information in one spot, including the property address, county where the property is located, the property type (residential, commercial, industrial, land, and so on), the tax parcel, legal description, and name and address of the current owner. You will be able to upload a photo of the property and add anything else you want.

Another great free feature from Google is Gmail, which can be tied into your Google Docs application. Gmail automatically adds addresses to your Contacts list each time you use the Reply, Reply to All, or Forward functions to send mail to addresses that don't already exist in your Contacts list. Each time you mark a message as *Not Spam*, your Contacts list is automatically updated so that future messages from that sender are received in your inbox.

Using Gmail and Google Docs, you can calendar important dates such as the date of purchase, the owner's redemption date, any foreclosure dates, additional tax due and other dates, and also generate automatic pop-up reminders so you never miss those dates. It is important to be well organized all the time because you will be able to operate in a more efficient manner.

## GENERATING REPORTS

One of the best features of using a good software tracking system is that you can generate and print as many different kinds of reports as you might need or want at any time on individual tax lien certificates and your entire real estate portfolio. For instance, you may want a list of all of the tax lien certificates owned, the ones that are redeemed or open, information on the county, a calendar of important dates, and so on. The number of reports you can generate is unlimited, and they will be extremely helpful in allowing you to make important financial decisions about your investment business. You need to be able to keep track of the following categories of information.

Quickly and easily record tax lien certificate information:

- **Property address**—The actual legal address where the property is located. This could be different from the address listed on the tax assessor's website, which might be just a PO Box.
- **County where the property resides**—The name of the county in the state where your property is located.
- **Type of property** (e.g., residential, commercial)—Is it a single family home? Duplex? Triplex? Quad? Strip mall?
- **Acreage**—Really important only when you are buying vacant land.
- **Tax parcel number and property number**—These can be found on the taxing authority's website and also on your receipt of purchase.
- **Section, township, and range information**—Not very important unless you plan on having a survey done of the property.
- **Owner information**—Highly important! This is the person/entity you want to keep in touch with to determine how this tax lien is going to play out.
- **Picture of property**—Not critical, but nice to have and easy to get from Google.
- **Place legal description and other notes**—Legal description is very important, as we discussed in earlier chapters. Make sure you have the correct legal description on file for any future foreclosure actions.

Enter significant dates:

- **Purchase date**—This is the actual date you purchased the tax certificate at the auction.
- **Redemption date**—Obviously extremely important. If you fail to keep track of anything else on this list, *do not forget* this date! It is the date you get paid!
- **Foreclosure date**—The date after the redemption period when you can legally file a foreclosure action to take title to the property.
- **Deed application date**—Depending on your state, this is the date when you applied for a tax deed for a property you foreclosed on, or the date the tax deed was issued to you.
- **Subsequent taxes due date**—When are the next taxes due? The last thing you ever want to happen is to take title to a property through a tax deed, then forget to pay the taxes on the property and have someone purchase the tax lien certificate on *your* property!
- **File tax deed date**—The date the tax deed was actually recorded by the county clerk.

Enter tax lien financial information:

- **Cost of lien**—How much you actually paid for the lien at the auction. This lets you know how much money you have invested in this certificate.
- **Face value of lien**—What the lien is worth when redeemed.
- **Enter subsequent costs incurred and dates**—Did you have to pay any subsequent taxes, filing or auction fees, and so on? Keep track of these amounts and dates, since they are write-offs on the eventual profit you make from the sale and therefore can be deducted on your tax return.
- **Land value**—Taken from the property assessor's website. What the actual vacant land is worth without any structures on it.
- **Improved value**—Taken from the property assessor's website. What the actual structures on the property are worth, not including the land.
- **Assessed value**—Taken from the property assessor's website. What the combined value of the vacant land and the structures is.
- **Fair market value**—Using your own research and tools or possibly a Realtor in the area, determine what the property would sell for today on the open market.
- **Accrual rate on tax certificate**—Interest you are earning on the tax lien.
- **Accrual basis: face value or premium**—Are you earning interest on the full amount, or was this a bid-down and the county is keeping part of the interest as a premium?
- **Accrual type: simple interest, compound interest, or flat rate**—How is your interest being calculated? Very important to know. Einstein said there is no force more powerful in the universe than compound interest.

Enter and maintain each county's contact and vital information:

- **Name of county**—Pretty obvious, but you'd be surprised how many people forget where they purchased a tax lien.
- **Address**—A must-have for communicating with the county on redemption periods and so on.
- **Phone number, fax, and county website**—Also a must-have for keeping track of your investment and for knowing when other sales are coming up that you may want to bid on in that county.
- **Contact person**—Someone you met at the auction and got to know a little bit and can call on when you need information.

- **Auction location**—Every county holds their auctions in different locations. Some could be in the courthouse, others in the county clerk's office. Keep track of where the auctions are held and in what room.
- **Auction registration information and date**—Highly important. If you need to register before an auction and fail to do so, then you will be unable to bid once you get there. Talk about a waste of time and money.
- **Newspaper information**—This is twofold. One, to keep track of when auctions are being posted in the paper, and two, to keep track of what paper you must use when you need to post notices for foreclosure or other legal matters.
- **Next auction date**—Not urgent, but nice to know so you can plan around it.
- **Property tax due dates**—Again, *pay the taxes* on property you owe. Many counties will give you a discount on taxes paid ahead of the final due date, so keeping track of this information is critical.
- **Bid method**—As we discussed earlier, is it an open bid, bid-down system, rotation system, or other method?
- **Payment type accepted**—Do you have to bring certified checks, cash, credit card? Nothing makes you look less professional than winning an auction and going to pay for it with a debit card and finding out that's not going to work.

Things to keep track of if you are acting as a landlord for a property:

- **Security deposits**—How much a tenant gave you when they signed the lease.
- **Lease terms**—How long is the lease for? If it is a multiple-year lease, does it call for an automatic rent raise after a certain time period?
- **Rent rolls**—If it is a multi-family property, then what is the overall rent being collected for the entire complex?
- **Rent due dates**—Not every tenant may have their rent due on the first of the month. Keep track of which tenants' rents are due on which dates.
- **Legal notices**—If a tenant wants to leave the property and they have to give you a 30-day notice, make sure you have this documented.
- **Expenses**—When are the taxes due, the utilities, and so on? Make sure you don't miss any of these important dates. The last thing you want is for your tenants to call you up screaming that the water was turned off because you forgot to pay a bill on time.

# TAKING ACTION

*Faith is taking the first step even when you don't see the whole staircase.*
— Martin Luther King Jr.

**B**y going through this book, you've taken the first step on the path to financial freedom. Now it's time to keep moving! When you hesitate, you often allow yourself or other naysayers to talk you out of exploring this gold mine. Don't cheat yourself out of the amazing investment potential and financial independence that lies ahead for you and your family.

So finalize your game plan and take control of your destiny. *Get going now!*

## WHAT TO DO NOW!

Start slowly, but set a date and time to get started. Just set aside three to five hours the first week to do some basic research, but make it consistent. Having a well-thought-out daily, weekly, and monthly plan and checklist to follow will keep you focused and help you avoid wasting time. Set your goals in increments and follow your schedule the best that you can without getting too distracted or sidetracked. By setting aside a certain amount of time at a regular time on a daily basis to work on your business, you will soon fall into a comfortable and natural business routine.

## THE COMPLETE 13-STEP CHECKLIST

If you are anything like me, I like a checklist of things that I can follow to guide me along the path and make sure I keep on track. Here's a quick recap and checklist of the action steps you need to start taking now. It's actually pretty simple when you just follow the blueprint that's been laid out for you.

### 1. Decide Where to Invest

If you want to invest in multiple locations, begin with one area and hone your technique before expanding. Laws and procedures vary from state to state and even from county to county within each state. All things being equal, start close to home to avoid unnecessary travel expenses.

Whatever you decide to do, I strongly suggest you do not try to tackle multiple jurisdictions at once. There is a learning curve for investing in tax liens and tax deeds, just as there is a learning curve for understanding any new venture. The more jurisdictions you decide to invest in when you are first starting out, you are multiplying your learning curve for each jurisdiction.

Also, as I said in an earlier chapter, you should stay close to home. Learn to farm your neighborhood and know it inside and out. Especially for your first few auctions, you want to have photos of the properties in front of you when you bid, and you should know just what that block looks like. It will give you an edge.

## 2. Decide How to Invest

Are you going to invest personally or as a corporation? Do you have the capital you need to invest? If not, consider working with another investor and splitting the profits. Also determine whether you'll go with a QRP or Self-Directed IRA to invest for retirement. Will you physically attend tax sales, take the online auction route, or perhaps buy directly with OTC properties? Make sure you have an investment plan ready with answers to these questions so that you're prepared to move forward efficiently with choices you've carefully evaluated.

I strongly recommend setting up some sort of corporation to run your investments. If you plan on investing only in tax liens and cashing out at the redemption period, then you can get by with just one company for all your tax lien investing. Call it *My Investments, Inc.* or name it after your dog (I have done that, by the way)—whatever suits your fancy.

If you are going to be investing in tax deeds, then I strongly recommend you set up a different company for each property address, or at least for a small group of addresses. I set up a separate new company for each group of one million dollars' worth of properties, or ones in close proximity. You may want one company called 123 Main St., Inc., another company called 444 Appletree Way, Inc., and so on. The reason for this is to get the maximum protection for each of your assets. For example, let's say you make one company for all your tax deeds. Then there is a serious accident on one of your properties and the company becomes liable for a million-dollar injury.

*All* of the company's assets can be used to satisfy that million-dollar judgment. So if the property the accident occurred on is only worth $150,000, any other properties that are owned by that corporation can be used to come up with the balance. But if all of your other properties are in their own corporations, then the absolute worst thing that can happen to you is you lose that one property and not your entire portfolio. Yes, there is more paperwork and accounting involved in keeping track of multiple corporations, but the peace of mind you get from it is priceless.

## 3. Decide How Much to Invest

Remember that your funds will be tied up, potentially for years, and take care not to invest money you may need in the meantime. With good research, you can determine and limit the timeframe of these investments, but they are not short-term plays. Contact the county to determine all the potential charges that could be included when you purchase a lien or deed. All these costs typically must be paid at the time of sale, so be prepared with the total amount needed.

There's an old saying "Never go gambling with the mortgage money." While investing in tax liens and tax deeds is far from gambling, as I've shown throughout this book, the general theory is the same. Do not invest funds that you may need to pay bills or unexpected expenses in the short-term because, as I've shown, these investments are not easy to liquidate. So how do you determine how much money you can safely invest? Here's a good formula for getting started.

Let's say your normal monthly expenses are $5,000 a month and your normal monthly income is $6,000 a month. This means that, over the course of a year, you can expect to save $12,000. Let's also say that right now you have $7,000 sitting in the bank in savings. What I advise people to do is calculate two months' worth of expenses and always keep that much available in a savings account as a financial insurance policy. That means even if you have zero money come in for two months, you can still pay all your expenses.

So two months' worth of money in your savings account would need to be $10,000. You already have $7,000 in the bank. Spend the next three months getting your savings up to $10,000 and, just as important, researching the market you are going to invest in and doing all of your pre-auction research and due diligence. Then once you have that $10,000 socked away, start investing the $1,000 a month you are making above and beyond your expenses.

This is a very safe way to determine how much to invest and when to start investing. You may want to take a bigger risk, say, keeping one month of expenses in the bank instead of two. The choice of course is yours. My goal is to protect you from yourself. After finishing this book, it is natural to want to take every dime you can find under your sofa cushions and start investing, because you are excited. While excitement is good and you should be excited about the new possibilities that have opened up for you, you also need to use common sense and keep some money in the bank for unexpected expenses.

## 4. Investment Strategy

If you are seeking a straight guaranteed profit, then you should focus on tax liens and the locations that might generate the greatest rate of return.

If acquiring the property is your goal, then tax deeds are a more effective investment vehicle.

Again, while you can invest in both of these vehicles when you first start out, it is better to pick one first and master it before moving on to another. Tax liens are the easiest to start out with; they have the smallest learning curves and almost no risk of losing money on your initial investment. It's a safe way to get your feet wet in tax lien investing.

## 5. Acquire the Tax Sale List

Contact the county for a list of delinquent properties available for sale, as well as the date and location of the sale. Consult the state and county guides in the appendix of this book for important dates, but always confirm with the county in case dates change. Also check local newspapers for notices of sale, or send out the preformatted letters we have provided you with. Remember to check for updates every few days before the sale in the event that property owners pay their taxes and properties are removed from the list.

The Internet is going to be your best friend. Check the county website regularly to see what changes have happened. But even better, find out who in the county is responsible for updating the website and send them some flowers. Sometimes the county may have information on hand and ready to publish, but it doesn't hit the website for a couple of days. A nice bouquet of flowers to the right person can get you some inside information and a jump on your competition.

## 6. Select Quality Properties

Focus on single-family residential properties whose value ratio (the percentage of back taxes owed versus value) is favorable. Start with specific types that you are familiar and comfortable with, then expand as you get more experience under your belt.

While you might be tempted to jump into the deep end of the pool and buy liens on corporate parks and industrial complexes, just relax. Those properties aren't going anywhere. Learn to walk before you run. Also, making a mistake on a $75,000 property is a lot easier to overcome then making a mistake on a $750,000 property. Start small, learn the ropes, and then expand into as many areas as you feel comfortable.

## 7. Conduct the Research

One of the most important steps for an investor is research. Always do your due diligence before dealing with any property venture. Tax deeds will require two to three times the amount of research that tax liens do. You can mine for information through sources and methods such as: local assessor's office, register of deeds, online real estate databases, maps, and of course, physical inspections.

When you are first starting out, look for tax liens on properties secured by a mortgage. The reason is, as I've shown you, that 99 percent of the time the mortgage company will redeem these liens so as not to lose the collateral on their loan, and your profit is guaranteed.

With tax deeds or any kind of real estate property investing, you must have your exit strategy in place before you purchase the property. You have to work backwards. This means you have to look at a piece of property, do all of your research and due diligence, and then ask yourself "What am I going to do with this property once I own it?" Your answer could be: immediately sell it, lease option it, rent it, fix it up and sell it at a premium, and so on. Just be sure to know what your plan is.

## 8. Prioritize Your List

You won't get them all! Having done your due diligence on listed properties and ensuring you have an updated list, prioritize your properties based on assessment value and market value, as well as on location and minimum bid prices. You may also want to prioritize them based on maximum interest rate allowed to be charged in that county, if you are going to be bidding on properties in multiple counties.

One of the easiest ways to prioritize your list is to go through it and cross out all the properties you know are dogs—those that your research has shown for one reason or another you are not going to bid on. Just having these properties off your page and out of sight will make the other properties stand out and help you organize them.

## 9. Set Your Limit

Do your homework on each property up for bid, so that you know the maximum price you're willing to pay and the minimum interest you're willing to accept. Know your maximums and minimums *and stick to them.* Jot down notes on your list prior to attending the sale, so you're aware of your limits.

Write yourself a note next to your maximum bid that says "Only an idiot would bid higher than this amount for this property." It's a nice way to motivate yourself to not get caught up in the excitement of the auction, and also a way for you to see someone else bid higher and, instead of feeling bad that you're not going to win the property, you can look at your note and then look at the other person and say, "Gee, I'm glad I'm not *that* idiot." These are the little mental games we have to play with ourselves to keep motivated and positive.

## 10. Get Ready, Get Set, Bid!

Remember to attend sales with your due diligence data and maximum bid limits in hand. Stay the course with what you've already decided to do. It's sometimes easy to get carried away in a competitive and sometimes charged environment. Do *not* let that happen to you. You've already charted your course, and you know what you need to do. Stick to the plan.

Also a reminder: if you are participating in an online auction, make sure you still keep printouts of all your information in front of you. Don't trust the computer to hold it all and be flipping back and forth from computer screens to auction screens. You are bound to either make a mistake or miss out on something, because you had the auction screen minimized while you were looking up data that should have been sitting right there on your desk.

I also like to keep copies of previous auctions, because the same properties have a way of coming back up for sale sometimes.

## 11. Arrange Payment

If you are a successful bidder, most auctions require that you be prepared to pay immediately. Ideally, you will have contacted the county to determine all possible costs prior to attending a sale. You may need to pay in cash, money order, or a cashier's check, so be prepared to pay the full amount of the bid, plus the associated costs. Bring cashier's checks in various denominations so that you are prepared for a variety of winning bids.

## 12. Track Your Investment

Establish a workable system for tracking your portfolio to avoid the risk of missing deadlines, notification requirements, redemption dates, and other actions that could have an impact on your return. Even a simple three-ring binder will work to start. Once you get going, you will want to acquire a software tracking system.

We've talked about the individual items you need to track in previous chapters, but this cannot be stressed enough. Miss a redemption date, or a hearing date, and you have lost out on your investment. Pen and paper or spreadsheet systems work great when you only have a few properties to keep track of, but I strongly suggest that once your portfolio contains more than 20 properties, especially if they are in different jurisdictions, you should invest in a tracking software program. This $100 software investment will be worth its weight in gold.

### 13. Do It Again!

Don't pin all your hopes on one piece of property. The beauty of tax sales is that there are precious few requirements for buyers. If you have the money to pay for a lien or deed, you can bid on it. Your credit is not an issue, there are no limits on how many properties you can purchase at one time, and you don't even have to be a citizen of the United States. So just as you might with any investment portfolio, diversify and give yourself every chance to profit. If one investment doesn't work out in quite the way you anticipated, you will have the reassurance of knowing that you have other properties that may come through and help offset any loss.

The true secret to any real estate investment strategy is to find something that works, and then repeat it 100 times. Don't try to reinvent the wheel. While it's okay to expand your tax portfolio and I encourage you to do so, don't try to be the man of all trades, master of none. You have everything you need to learn in this book to make money buying tax liens and tax deeds. Learn it, do it, repeat it. Don't get distracted by other investors who tell you, "I've made three million dollars this year buying only short sales!" You may start thinking to yourself, "Hmm, I could use three million dollars." I'm telling you it's a trap.

What you're not hearing is that it took your friends two years of learning how short sales work before they started making money. Don't jump around, because the grass is not always greener on the other property. Sticking with what you know will make you money. Tax sales are held every single day all across the country. Once you've got the hang of it, all you need to do is simply rinse and repeat!

## MEASURING YOUR SUCCESS

*Knowledge is not power or success, it's the application of knowledge that is the real power of success.*

—*Jim Rohn*

One way to measure your success is to track how many tax liens and tax deeds you have acquired. Another measurement that you can use once you start building your portfolio is to look at how many of your tax lien certificates have been redeemed and paid to you. Have you generated a positive monthly cash flow and are you seeing a consistent return on your investments? Take a look at the properties you have acquired through foreclosure. Are they generating rental income and positive cash flow? Have you recouped your rehab and investment costs when you sold them? Are you using your time wisely? How many new lists of tax lien certificates and tax deed auctions have you added to your tracking system? How many auctions are you attending each month? These answers will give you important insight into how you are doing so you know what areas you can improve and where you are exceeding.

## SETTING GOALS AND EVALUATING RESULTS

Set realistic goals that you can meet. Keep them in increments. Tell yourself, "This month I am going to buy one tax lien certificate." Then take all of the steps necessary to make that happen. The absolute worst thing you can do is nothing. Making a mistake is better than doing nothing! Success does not happen overnight. It's a product of many small steps taken one after the other that, at the time, don't seem very important, but they act like a boulder rolling downhill. They gain momentum as they go, and soon they are an unstoppable force of progress you have made toward achieving your goals. If you don't know how to set goals, then start with this simple suggestion. Tell yourself, "Today I am going to spend one hour doing *something* to learn more about tax liens and tax deeds." Just doing something every day will get the boulder rolling for you, and then the goals will start setting themselves.

You may have to reset or adjust your goals as you go along. This way you won't become frustrated—you will see results even if they are small. Eventually the small results will help you reach your long-term goals. Use your checklists and keep striving to improve your results. Remember, tax lien and tax deed investing is a learning process and, like everything else in life, it takes time to perfect and reach the results and goals that you have set for yourself.

## FINAL THOUGHTS

You now have all the information you need to create long-term wealth for you and your family. Just follow the steps, and make a commitment to do it! I have tried to share my years' worth of experience so that you don't make the same mistakes I did, and you can start out profitably right from the start.

Good things don't come to those who wait, they come to those who hustle. Just go do it. By sending out your county letters, keeping track of upcoming auctions, and doing your research, you'll not only make a nice profit, but you'll be meeting some incredible people, visiting some exciting places, and building a future.

I want to personally thank you for spending some time with me, and I trust that you found it was time well spent. I invite you to contact me with any questions, problems, and of course, all the success stories that you have. My e-mail is Chip@ChipCummings.com, and my office phone number is (866) 977-7900.

Be sure to go to my website and register to receive all the downloadable forms, checklists, and letters, and to find out about upcoming auctions. It's all free to you as a way to say thanks for your time and commitment. Just go to www.ZeroRiskRealEstate.com/Bonus for details.

My best wishes to you and your dreams, and I'll see you on the Road to Success—with *Zero Risk*!

# APPENDIX A

# 101 ONLINE RESOURCES

To help you out with your tax lien and tax deed investing, here is a list of resources and websites that my students and I have used. Remember, websites and companies can change, so for an updated list, visit: www.ZeroRiskRealEstate.com/Bonus.

### Online Tax Auction Sites

| | |
|---|---|
| Tax Sales and More | www.Bid4Assets.com |
| Auction Site (Indiana) | www.SRI-Taxsale.com |
| Auction Site (various) | www.RealAuction.com |
| Auction Site (various) | www.GrantStreet.com |
| Auction Site (Michigan) | www.Tax-Sale.info |
| Auction Site (Illinois) | www.ILTaxSale.com |

There are many other individual sites. For a complete up-to-date listing, check the ZRRE Resource Center. Make sure to do a search for county GIS maps as well.

### Maps and Aerial Photography

| | |
|---|---|
| Google | www.Maps.Google.com |
| MapQuest | www.MapQuest.com |
| Aerial Maps | www.terraserver.com/ |
| Google Earth | www.Earth.Google.com |
| Yahoo! Maps | www.Maps.Yahoo.com |
| Bing | www.Bing.com/maps |

### Foreclosure Properties and Statistics

| | |
|---|---|
| Foreclosure Statistics | www.RealtyTrac.com |
| HUD Homes for Sale | www.hud.gov/homes/homesforsale.cfm |
| Government Homes for Sale | http://homesales.gov/homesales/main Action.do |

| | |
|---|---|
| Foreclosure Search | www.ForeclosureFreeSearch.com |
| Foreclosure Listings | www.ForeclosureListings.com |
| Foreclosure Listings | www.Foreclosures.com |
| Illinois Foreclosures | www.public-record.com/content/ databases/foreclosures/index.asp |
| San Diego Foreclosures | www.ForeclosureAccess.com |
| Foreclosure Records | http://records.foreclosure.com/ |

Use these to research a property history for a tax sale. In addition, many lenders and banks have individual pages listing REO properties for sale.

### Approximate Property Values

| | |
|---|---|
| Zillow Property Valuation | www.Zillow.com |
| Realtor Sales/Listings | www.Realtor.com |
| Multiple Listing Search | www.MLS.com |
| MLS – Canada | www.MLS.ca |
| House Values | www.HouseValues.com |
| Trulia | www.Trulia.com |
| Yahoo! Home Values | http://realestate.yahoo.com/Homevalues |

Local real estate agents will always be the best source of current local market conditions and values.

### Association and Regulatory Agencies

| | |
|---|---|
| Mortgage Bankers Association | www.MBAA.org |
| Mortgage Brokers Association | www.NAMB.org |
| National Association of Realtors® | www.Realtor.com |
| Fannie Mae | www.FannieMae.com |
| Freddie Mac | www.FreddieMac.com |
| FHA | www.HUD.gov |
| US Department of Veteran Affairs | www.VA.gov |
| National NREIA | www.NationalREIA.com |
| Rental Property Managers | www.NARPM.org |
| US Government info site | www.USA.gov |

### Public Property Records

| | |
|---|---|
| Government Records | www.brbpub.com/freeresources/pubrecsites .aspx |
| Virtual Gumshoe | www.VirtualGumshoe.com |
| Public Record Finder | www.PublicRecordFinder.com |
| Search Systems | www.SearchSystems.com |

| Yellow/White Pages | www.Switchboard.com |
| Public Records | www.OnlineSearches.com |
| Public Records Search | www.PRSearch.com |
| Bankruptcy Records | http://pacer.psc.uscourts.gov/ |
| Chapter 13 Records | www.13DataCenter.com |
| Tax Records Search | www.Netronline.com/public_records.htm |

Most state, county, and city recorder's offices also have records online.

### People Searches

| Intelius Search | www.Intelius.com |
| Accurint | www.Accurint.com |
| Web Detective | www.Web-Detective.com |
| ZabaSearch | www.ZabaSearch.com |
| People Search | www.People-Search.com |
| Zoom | www.ZoomInfo.com |
| Lycos People Search | www.WhoWhere.com |
| Skip Ease | www.SkipEase.com |
| Social Security Administration | www.SSA.gov |

### Demographic Information

| Cost of Living Statistics | www.BestPlaces.net |
| US Geocode Info | www.ffiec.gov/Geocode/default.aspx |
| Census Information | www.Census.gov/ |
| Federal Statistics | www.fedstats.gov/ |
| Labor Statistics | www.BLS.gov |
| Federal Housing Oversight | www.fhfa.gov/ |

### Crime Information

| US Dept of Justice | www.ojp.usdoj.gov/bjs/ |
| FBI Crime Reports | www.FBI.gov/ucr/ucr.htm |
| State Crime Statistics | www.bestplaces.net/crime/ |
| City Crime Statistics | www.Melissadata.com/lookups/crimecity.asp |
| National Sex Offender Registry | www.FBI.gov/hq/cid/cac/registry.htm |

### Attorney and Legal Resources

| Lawyer Search | www.FindLaw.com |
| Legal Questions | www.LawGuru.com |
| Legal Forms | www.LegalZoom.com |

| Free Forms and Research | www.LawInfo.com |
| Attorney Search | www.lawyers.com |

**Title Insurance Research**

| First American | www.FirstAm.com |
| Property Records | www.firstam.com/list |
| | .cfm?id=70&sectionid=05 |
| Stewart Title | www.Stewart.com |
| Old Republic Title | www.OldRepublicTitle.com |
| Chicago Title | https://www.ctic.com/ |
| Fidelity National | https://www.fntic.com/ |

These are the major title insurers. There are many agents located throughout the country, including in many attorney offices.

**Appraisal Resources**

| Appraisal Institute | www.appraisalinstitute.org/ |
| Appraiser Search | www.isa-appraisers.org/ISA_form.html |
| Appraisers Forum | www.AppraisersForum.com |
| HUD Appraisal Guidelines | www.hud.gov/offices/hsg/sfh/ref/chap1 |
| | .cfm |

**Rehabilitation and Repair Costs**

| Construction Calculators | www.construction-resource.com/ |
| | calculators/ |
| Lowe's Job Estimator | www.lowesforpros.com/ |
| | BlueprintEstimates |
| Quote Estimator | www.get-a-quote.net/quickcalc/ |
| Marshall Swift | http://marshallswift.com/ |
| RS Means | www.RSMeans.com |
| Geometric Calculator | www.Blocklayer.mobi |

**Tax Information**

| Federal Tax Information | www.IRS.gov |
| Tax Search | www.Netronline.com/public_records.htm |
| Tax and Assessor Search | www.knowx.com/subreg/pr_assets.jsp |
| Maryland Tax Search | www.dat.state.md.us/ |
| Miami-Dade Tax Search | www.miamidade.gov/proptax/ |
| El Paso, Texas | https://actweb.acttax.com/act_webdev/ |
| | elpaso/index.jsp |

Several regional examples are listed above. Most tax searches are done at the local county or city level. Check with your tax assessor or treasurer's office for their website access address.

### Environmental Resources

| | |
|---|---|
| Environmental Protection Agency | www.epa.gov/osw |
| Superfund Sites | www.epa.gov/superfund/ |
| Pollution Statistics | www.Scorecard.org |
| Environmental Sites | www.World.org/weo/pollution |
| Lead-Based Paint Info | www.epa.gov/lead/ |
| Lead Disclosure Rule | www.hud.gov/offices/lead/ enforcement/disclosure.cfm |

### Other Resource Sites

| | |
|---|---|
| Credit Reports | www.AnnualCreditReport.com |
| Do Not Call List | www.DoNotCall.gov |
| Mortgage Payment Calculator | www.bankrate.com/brm/ mortgage-calculator.asp |
| 100 Mortgage Calculators | www.mortgageloan.com/ calculator/ |
| US Zip Code Registry | https://tools.usps.com/go/ ZipLookupAction!input.action |

# APPENDIX B

# STATE LISTINGS

H ere is a list of state tax lien and tax deed regulations, interest rates, and code references. For a complete listing of counties in each state with contact information, interest rates, and sale dates, please go to the resource center at: www.ZeroRiskRealEstate.com/Bonus.

| State | Type | Interest | Redemption | Website |
|---|---|---|---|---|
| ALABAMA | Lien | 12% | 3 years | www.ador.state.al.us |
| ALASKA | Deed | - | None | http://www.alaska.gov/ |
| ARIZONA | Lien | 16% | 3 years | www.azdor.gov |
| ARKANSAS | Deed | - | 1–3 years | www.arkansas.gov/acd/index.html |
| CALIFORNIA | Deed | - | 1 year | www.boe.ca.gov/index.htm |
| COLORADO | Lien | Fed + 9% | 3 years | www.colorado.gov/revenue |
| CONNECTICUT | Lien | 18% | 6 months | www.ct.gov/drs/site/default.asp |
| DELAWARE | Deed | 15% | 60 days | www.finance.delaware.gov/ |
| FLORIDA | Lien | 18% | 2 years | http://dor.myflorida.com/dor |
| GEORGIA | Lien | 20% | 1 year | http://dor.georgia.gov |
| HAWAII | Deed | 12% | 1 year | www.state.hi.us/tax/tax.html |
| IDAHO | Deed | - | - | http://tax.idaho.gov |
| ILLINOIS | Lien | 18–48% | 2–3 years | http://www.iltax.com/#t=tab1 |
| INDIANA | Lien | 10–30% | 1 year | http://www.ai.org/dor |
| IOWA | Lien | 24% | 2 years | www.iowa.gov/tax |
| KANSAS | Deed | - | 2 years | www.ksrevenue.org |
| KENTUCKY | Lien | 12% | 1 year | http://revenue.ky.gov |
| LOUISIANA | Lien | 12% + | 3 years | www.rev.state.la.us |
| MAINE | Deed | - | - | www.state.me.us/revenue/homepage.html |
| MARYLAND | Lien | 6% + | Varies | www.comp.state.md.us |
| MASSACHUSETTS | Lien | 16% | Varies | www.mass.gov |
| MICHIGAN | Deed | - | - | http://michigan.gov/taxes |
| MINNESOTA | Deed | - | - | http://www.state.mn.us |
| MISSISSIPPI | Lien | 18% + | 2 years | www.dor.ms.gov |
| MISSOURI | Lien | 10% | 2 years | http://dor.mo.gov |
| MONTANA | Lien | 10% + | 3 years | http://revenue.mt.gov/default.mcpx |

| State | Type | Interest | Redemption | Website |
|---|---|---|---|---|
| NEBRASKA | Lien | 14% | 3 years | www.revenue.state.ne.us |
| NEVADA | Deed | - | - | http://tax.state.nv.us/ |
| NEW HAMPSHIRE | Lien | 18% | 2 years | www.nh.gov/revenue/index.htm |
| NEW JERSEY | Lien | 18% + | 2 years | www.state.nj.us/treasury/taxation |
| NEW MEXICO | Deed | - | - | www.tax.newmexico.gov |
| NEW YORK | Both | 12% | 2 years | www.tax.state.ny.us |
| NORTH CAROLINA | Deed | - | - | www.dor.state.nc.us |
| NORTH DAKOTA | Deed | - | - | www.nd.gov/tax |
| OHIO | Both | 18% | 1 year | http://tax.ohio.gov |
| OKLAHOMA | Deed | - | - | www.ok.gov/section.php?sec_id=49 |
| OREGON | Deed | - | - | www.oregon.gov/dor/scd/index.shtml |
| PENNSYLVANIA | Deed | - | - | www.revenue.state.pa.us |
| PUERTO RICO | Lien | 20% | 1 year | www2.pr.gov/Pages/default.aspx |
| RHODE ISLAND | Lien | 10% + | 1 year | www.tax.state.ri.us |
| SOUTH CAROLINA | Lien | 12% + | 1 year | www.sctax.org/default.htm |
| SOUTH DAKOTA | Lien | 10% | 3 years | www.state.sd.us/drr2/revenue.html |
| TENNESSEE | Deed | 10% | 1 year | www.state.tn.us/revenue |
| TEXAS | Deed | 25% + | Varies | www.window.state.tx.us |
| UTAH | Deed | - | - | http://tax.utah.gov |
| VERMONT | Deed | 12% | 1 year | www.state.vt.us/tax/index.shtml |
| VIRGINIA | Deed | - | - | www.tax.virginia.gov |
| VIRGIN ISLANDS | Lien | 12% | 1 year | www.governordejongh.com |
| WASHINGTON | Deed | - | - | http://dor.wa.gov |
| WASH DC | Lien | 18% | 6 months | http://cfo.dc.gov/cfo/site/default.asp |
| WEST VIRGINIA | Lien | 12% | 18 months | www.wv.gov/residents/Pages/taxes.aspx |
| WISCONSIN | Deed | - | - | www.dor.state.wi.us/ |
| WYOMING | Lien | 15% + | 4 years | http://revenue.state.wy.us |

# GLOSSARY

Real estate investors, counties, and lenders have a language all their own. In this glossary, we present and decipher the most cryptic jargon and acronyms you are likely to encounter.

**1031**   See Tax-deferred exchange.

**Abatement**   The reduction, decrease, or elimination of a tax previously assessed.

**Absentee Bidding**   A process by which a bid may be submitted without the presence of the person submitting it, such as: by mail, by phone, by an assistant, etc.

**Abstract (aka Abstract of Title)**   1. A condensed history of the chain of title to land, including, but not limited to, a statement of all liens, charges, encumbrances, and liabilities the land is subject to. May also include maps and plats. 2. In Texas, the book or volume of plat maps is sometimes known as an Abstract.

**Acre**   A measurement of land in any shape equivalent to 43,560 square feet (160 sq. rods). 640 acres make up a section, 36 sections make up a township.

**Adjusted Basis**   Value used in calculating the taxable gain on the sale of a property. The adjusted basis is the original cost of the property plus capital improvements, minus accumulated depreciation and the cost of selling it.

**Adjustment Period**   The length of time that determines how often the interest rate can change on an adjustable rate mortgage. See also Index, Cap, and Margin.

**Ad Valorem**   Taxes imposed at a rate set by law or as a percentage of value.

**Amortization**   Creative process of retiring debt through predetermined periodic payments.

**Appraisal**   Evaluation or estimation of value of property by disinterested persons of suitable qualifications.

**Appreciation**   Increase in the market value of real estate over its value since purchase.

**APR (Annual Percentage Rate)**   Calculation disclosed on the Truth-in-Lending Act (TIL), which indicates the total cost of credit when other costs are taken into account.

**ARM (Adjustable Rate Mortgage)**   A mortgage in which the interest rate can change.

**Assessed Value**   A value set by local government appraisers under the guidelines of state statute for the express purpose of property taxation.

**Assignment Purchasing**   The transfer of a lien position from a government entity to a private investor. More simply stated, property liens not sold at auction are offered *over-the-counter* for purchase at a later date.

**AU (Automated Underwriting)**   Computerized system used by lenders to determine a borrower's eligibility for loan programs.

**AVM (Automated Valuation Model)**   A computerized system for determining the value of a property that can take the place of an appraisal.

**Back-End Debt Ratio**   Total debt payments (including monthly house payment plus homeowner's insurance and property taxes) divided by total monthly income. According to the Federal Housing Authority (FHA), your back-end debt ratio should not exceed 43 percent. See also Debt ratio and Front-end debt ratio.

**Balloon Payment**   A typically large final payment due on a loan that covers the remaining balance. Balloon payments are required when a loan is scheduled to be paid in full before the debt can be retired through monthly payments.

**Bankruptcy**   Proceedings against a debtor, who has been declared legally insolvent, to distribute the debtor's property among the creditors.

**Baseline**   Survey line used to establish township lines on a map grid. The baseline runs east and west on the grid in order to establish north and south halves of the grid.

**Basis**   The starting point for calculating the gain or loss on an investment—usually the purchase price.

**Bidding a Premium or Bonus Amount**   The bidding for any particular lien at auction begins at the total amount of delinquent taxes, plus interest accrued, penalties, and any other costs. The successful bidder is the one who offers the largest cash amount in excess of the amount due on the tax lien.

**Bidding Down on a Percentage of Ownership (aka Bidding down the interest in a property)**   The bidding for any particular lien at auction begins at the maximum interest rate allowed by law. Investors offer bids in a declining manner (such as first 16, then 15, then 14 percent, etc.).

The successful bidder is that investor who is willing to accept the least amount of interest for his/her investment.

**Bid in (aka Bid Off)**  A phrase used to describe the process whereby liens or properties are not sold at auction but are written off to the county for disposition.

**BPO**  Broker Price Opinion. An informal estimate of value used for helping the lender determine the current value of a foreclosure property.

**CAP**  The maximum interest rate allowed for an Adjustable Rate Mortgage loan.

**Capital**  Money used for investing purposes.

**Capital Gain or Loss**  The net profit on an investment property that is subject to tax. Capital gains can be long-term (taxed at a lower rate) or short-term, depending on how long the property is held by any one owner.

**Capital Improvement**  A renovation that increases the value or useful life of a property for a period in excess of one year.

**Cartographer**  A maker of maps. Usually it is a department within the assessor's office, or a freestanding county department committed to the creation and maintenance of government plat and subdivision maps.

**Cash Flow**  The net operating income (NOI) of a property minus its debt service. See also NOI and DS.

**Cause Number**  An index number assigned by the Clerk of the Court to lawsuits filed in civil court actions. The first two digits of the number usually identify the calendar year in which the original motion is filed, usually followed by a dash, then a series of five or six digits that identify the individual case.

**Caveat Emptor**  Latin term for *Let the Buyer Beware*.

**C, C, & R'S**  Covenants, Conditions, and Restrictions. Guidelines set forth in a subdivision plan by a developer of the land.

**Certificate of Purchase**  See Tax Lien Certificate.

**Closing**  A ritual that involves all the parties to a real estate sale, who must meet and sign documents, disburse funds, and transfer ownership of the real estate.

**Closing Costs**  Costs incurred by a purchaser of real estate, or paid on his/her behalf, to complete the closing of the transaction. Listed on the GFE (Good Faith Estimate) and the HUD-1.

**CLTV (Combined Loan To Value)**  The total percentage of Loan to Value with all mortgages included.

**Commercial Property**  Property used for business as opposed to living quarters. Technically, however, the term also covers residential real estate having five units or more.

**Comparable or Comps** Properties used as comparisons to determine the value of a like property. When appraising the value of a property by comparing the price of similar, recently sold properties, important things to remember are the degree of similarity and the circumstances of sale.

**Compound Interest** Interest calculated against the sum of the principal amount plus interest that has previously accrued.

**Condemnation** The legal process by which the right of Eminent Domain is exercised. Part of this process includes determining *just compensation*.

**Conforming Loan** A loan that adheres to all Fannie Mae and Freddie Mac requirements. See also Sub-prime loan.

**Contiguous Parcel** A neighboring or adjoining parcel of land, which may be in actual close contact, touching at a point or along a boundary of another property.

**Contract for Deed** See Land contract.

**Conventional Loan** A loan that doesn't require underwriting or insuring by the government (such as FHA or VA underwriting).

**Conveyance** The transfer of title to land from one person or persons to another by written instrument (such as a deed).

**Cost Approach** An appraisal method that starts with what it would cost to build the same structure today, depreciates it, and then adds in the value of the land.

**County Constant** The percentage of Fair Market Value that local assessors appraise property at for taxation purposes. This percentage is never mandated by statute. It is simply a rule of thumb used in order to simplify administration of the taxation process. For example, Arizona county assessors strive to assess property at 82 percent of Fair Market Value.

**County Index Map** 1. The general map of the county with a superimposed index relating to the parcel identification number. 2. A county map identifying the range and township designations of that county.

**Cross-Collateralization** Using two or more properties as security for the repayment of a loan.

**Debt Ratio** A formula that lenders often use to determine a borrower's ability to afford monthly payments on a loan. See also Back-end debt ratio and Front-end debt ratio.

**Deed** A written instrument transferring title of real property from one entity to another. Types of Deeds: Bargain and Sale Deed—Used in the conveyance of land title, when the purchase is made for valuable consideration (not cash). Contract for Sale Deed—An agreement by a seller to deliver conveyance of title upon completion of certain conditions (payments). Often used in place of a Warranty Deed when a purchase is subject to a particular claim. Quitclaim Deed—Transfers any title, interest, or claim a grantor may have in a property. Sheriff's Deed—(aka Constable's Deed) Usually issued at the order of a court judgment by a county law enforcement officer. Special Warranty Deed—Used to convey title of land in unique situations, such as multiple sellers with varying percentages of ownership to multiple buyers with varying percentages of ownership. It is limited to certain persons and/or claims. Tax Deed—(aka Auditor's Deed) Transfers the title of land taken for delinquent taxes to a purchaser at a public sale. Trust Deed—See Deed of Trust. Warranty Deed—A deed used in many states to convey fee title to real property. Prior to the common use of title insurance, a Warranty Deed expressed a guarantee that the title was free from defects.

**Deed of Trust**   An instrument now used in most states in place of a mortgage. The legal title to real property is transferred to a trustee in favor of the lender (aka beneficiary) until the borrower satisfies the terms of the contract.

**Depreciation**   The decline in value of a property over time, usually due to wear and tear.

**Discount Rate**   Rate that is used by banks and financial institutions when lending money among themselves. Sometimes used as an index for ARM loan adjustments.

**Due Diligence**   To take on the responsibility of performing one's own research to determine quality and/or value of a particular investment.

**Due on Sale Clause**   Wording in most mortgages that requires the borrower to pay the balance in full in the event that the property changes hands.

**Easement**   1. The right to use the property of another for a specific purpose, such as: for the benefit of a contiguous landowner so that he can get from parcel A to parcel B. 2. *Gross easement* as in a right-of-way for utility lines. Refers to the actual land used.

**Egress**   1. The path by which a person exits land. 2. The act or right of going or leaving. Often used with the term *ingress* in the combination *ingress and egress* (i.e., entering and leaving), which simply stated means the right to come and go across the land of another.

**EMD (Earnest Money Deposit)**   Funds put up by a prospective purchaser as a commitment to follow through on the purchase of a property.

**Eminent Domain**   The power to take private property for public use by federal, state, or local governments. This power is granted by the Fifth Amendment of the US Constitution. The taking of property by this device requires just compensation.

**Encumbrance**   A claim, lien, charge, or liability attached and/or binding to real property.

**Equity**   The amount of money remaining if you sold the property today and paid off any loans taken out against the property.

**Escheat**   A reversion of ownership of property (real or personal) to the state when there is a lack of any individual to inherit it.

**Estoppel Certificate**   Legal document that tenants use to acknowledge agreements or changes in the lease or the status of rent payments.

**Fair Market Value**   The appraised value of a property as compared with other property values on the market.

**Fee Simple**   1. Typically, the words *fee simple* standing alone create an absolute estate, or one without limitations and/or conditions. Those words followed by a condition or limitation are subject to those situations. 2. A synonym for ownership.

**FHA (Federal Housing Administration)**   The division of the Department of Housing and Urban Development that insures home mortgage loans.

**FICO (Fair Isaac & Company) score**   A credit scoring system commonly used by lenders to determine the risk a borrower represents related to repayment.

**FIFA**   A term used exclusively in Georgia, referring to a tax lien document or writ that authorizes the sheriff to obtain satisfaction of unpaid taxes by levying on and selling the delinquent taxpayer's property.

**Final Disposition Sale**   A term exclusive to Florida. After the expiration of the redemption period, tax liens in Florida are brought to a secondary sale to afford additional investors the opportunity to bid for the deed. The opening bid equals the redemption cost of the tax lien certificate. Should there be no additional bids, the lien holder is awarded the deed in exchange for the Certificate of Purchase.

**Financing**   The way in which an investor acquires the capital with which to purchase a property.

**Fixed-Rate Loan**   A loan for which the interest rate remains unchanged over the life of the loan. See also ARM.

**Foreclosure**   1. To destroy an equity of redemption. A termination of rights to real property. 2. To deprive an interested party of his rights to real estate.

**Forfeiture Clause**   Legal wording commonly used in a land contract or lease option agreement that entitles the seller to repossess the property in the event that the buyer fails to comply with the terms of the agreement.

**Front-End Debt Ratio**   House payment alone (including property taxes and insurance) divided by total monthly income. According to the FHA, your front-end debt ratio should not exceed 31 percent. See also Debt ratio and Back-end debt ratio.

**GFE (Good Faith Estimate)**   A list of estimated costs involved in a loan transaction that the lender provides to the borrower prior to, or within three days of, an application.

**Goal**   A purpose or objective that an individual is willing to work toward.

**Grantee**   One to whom a grant is made. Generally, the buyer.

**Grantor**   One who grants property to another. Generally, the seller.

**Hard Money**   A typically short-term, high-interest loan that investors often use to acquire some quick cash so that they can move forward on an investment opportunity.

**HELOC (Home Equity Line Of Credit)**   Credit line secured by a piece of real property. With an HELOC, you pay interest on only the amount of money you actually draw against the credit line.

**Homestead Exemption**   A reduction in the taxable value of a property as authorized by law. It can have different definitions in different states.

**HUD (Department of Housing and Urban Development)**   The branch of the federal government that oversees FHA.

**HUD-1**   Settlement statement used at closing to disclose all costs and credits for borrowers and sellers involved in a real estate transaction.

**Hybrid Loan**   A combination of an ARM and a fixed-rate loan; for example, with a 3/1 hybrid, the interest rate would remain fixed for three years and then become an adjustable-rate loan in which the rate could be adjusted every year. See also ARM and Fixed-rate loan.

**Improvement**   Buildings or other structures that become part of the land.

**In Arrears**   Delinquent.

**Income Approach**   A real estate appraisal method that focuses more on the revenue-generating potential of rental property than on the property's value.

**Incorporate**   The process of forming a local political body, such as a city or town, to create a municipal system.

**Index**   An indicator used to calculate rates on some mortgage loan products, notably ARM loans. See also Adjustment period, Cap, and Margin.

**Index Map**   A map of a taxing jurisdiction containing references to a tax identification numbering system.

**Ingress**   1. Access or entrance. 2. The act or right of entering. Often used with the term *egress* in the combination *ingress and egress* (i.e., entering and leaving), which simply stated means the right to come and go across the land of another.

**Interest**   A percentage of an amount of money paid for its use over a specific time frame. Usually expressed as an annual percentage of the amount of the loan.

**IRA**   Individual Retirement Account.

**Judgment**   The verdict of a court on a matter presented to it.

**Junior Lien**   A mortgage or other encumbrance with a secondary interest.

**Land Contract**   A legal instrument that enables a seller to finance the purchase of his property. The seller functions as the lender, and the contract takes the place of a mortgage or deed of trust.

**Lease**   A contractual agreement between the owner and the tenant, which allows the tenant to use and occupy a property for a specific period of time.

**Leasee**   One who contracts to hold occupancy rights in the real property of another.

**Lease Option Agreement**   A legal instrument that enables a buyer to rent a property for a certain amount of time, at the end of which she has the option to purchase it for the pre-agreed-upon price.

**Legal Description**   The means by which a property is identified through exact boundaries. The surveyor will use the recorded plats, metes and bounds, or the government survey to describe real property.

**Leverage**   The use of borrowed money to increase purchasing power.

**Lien**   1. A claim, encumbrance, or change on a property for payment of some debt. 2. Security for a debt. 3. The right to retain property for payment of a debt, in our case tax debt.

**Lien Certificate**   See Tax lien certificate.

**Lis Pendens**   1. Latin term for *a suit pending*, which refers to a written notice that a lawsuit has been filed which concerns real property. 2. A common law doctrine filed in court as notice of jurisdiction, power, or control a court will require over property in litigation, pending action and until final judgment.

**LLC (Limited Liability Company)**   A legal structure that protects the owner's personal assets from any loss that the business incurs.

**Loan Officer**   Someone who works for a lending institution or mortgage broker to assist borrowers in selecting and applying for loans. See also Mortgage broker.

**Long-Term Capital Gain**   The realized profit on an investment property held more than 12 months.

**LTV (Loan-To-Value)**   A ratio expressing the loan amount divided by the property's current market value. For example, the LTV on an $80,000 loan to purchase a $100,000 property would be 80 percent. Lenders use LTV as one way to measure risk—the lower the LTV, the less the risk.

**Management Expenses (ME)** Whatever you pay yourself or others to care for a property.

**Margin** An amount added to an index to calculate an adjustment for an ARM loan. The margin remains constant over the life of the loan. See also Adjustment period, Index, and Cap.

**Maturity** The date on which the principal amount of a note, draft, bond, lien, or other debt instrument becomes due and payable.

**Meridian** Survey line used to establish range lines on a map grid. The meridian runs north and south on the grid in order to establish east and west halves of the grid.

**Mill** The rate of tax imposed upon taxable value. One mill equals $1 of tax for every $1,000 of taxable value.

**Minimum Bid** The opening price a property will be offered for at auction. See also Opening bid.

**Mortgage** A loan secured by real estate. States which are not trust states use a mortgage as the legal instrument to secure a lien against the property.

**Mortgage Broker** A licensed professional who assists borrowers in shopping for loans made available through multiple lenders.

**MUD** Municipal Utilities District. A type of taxing jurisdiction.

**Net Worth** The value of everything you own minus everything you owe.

**NOI (Net Operating Income)** The amount of money left over after all expenses are deducted from a property's gross income.

**Non-Conforming Loan** See Sub-prime loan.

**Note** Legal instrument that describes the terms of the mortgage loan.

**Opening Bid** 1. The beginning bid of an item at auction. Generally, the amount of all taxes, interest, penalties, and fees. 2. The first bid. See also Minimum bid.

**Operating Expenses** Costs for maintaining a property, such as taxes, insurance, maintenance, and upkeep.

**Over-the-Counter List** 1. A list of liens/properties available for sale after an auction has taken place. These liens/properties can be purchased with no competitive bidding and as an arms-length transaction. They are sold on a first come, first served basis.

**Parcel** 1. A contiguous area of land described in a single description by a deed or other instrument. 2. A number of lots on a plat or plan, separately owned and capable of being separately conveyed.

**Pass-Through Expenses** Costs that a landlord incurs and then charges the tenant to pay in full or a portion of, in addition to paying rent.

**Penalty** A sum of money attached to a debt as a punishment for nonpayment.

**Per Annum** By the year; annually; yearly.

**Personal Property**   1. In a general sense, everything subject to owner-ship that is not considered to be real property. 2. Movable assets. For taxa-tion purposes, some examples would be: a dentist's chair, farm machinery, a mobile home, hotel furniture, and so on.

**PIN or PID**   Parcel Identification Number (aka Parcel Number), (aka Property Number), (aka Account Number), (aka Abstract Number), (aka Folio Number), etc.

**PITI (Principal + Interest + Taxes + Insurance)**   Term used to describe a payment that covers the principal and interest due on a loan along with taxes and insurance to be placed in escrow.

**Plat Map (aka Subdivision Map)**   A map outlining individual lots within a block or tract of land.

**PMI (Private Mortgage Insurance)**   Insurance required on high LTV conventional loans.

**Points**   Interest paid on a loan up front rather than monthly. One point is one percent of the total loan amount.

**Pre-Approval**   A lender's agreement to finance the purchase of an invest-ment property up to a certain amount, assuming the property meets certain conditions. See also Prequalification.

**Premium**   The difference between the purchase price and the opening/minimum bid of a property at auction.

**Premium Bidding**   An opening bid that equals the sum of taxes, interest, and penalties due. Bidding continues in set dollar amount increments, increasing with each new bid.

**Prepaids**   Costs of a transaction listed on the GFE or HUD-1, which are paid in advance for the benefit of the borrower.

**Prepayment Penalty**   A clause in some mortgage agreements that requires the borrower to pay additional money if she pays back the loan early.

**Prequalification**   A lender's assurance that a borrower probably would qualify for a particular loan. See also Pre-approval.

**Pro Forma**   A statement projecting the future performance of an income-producing property.

**Promissory Note**   A legal document borrowers sign as their personal agreement to pay back a loan according to the terms specified in the note.

**Property ID Number**   A county treasurer's way of identifying a particu-lar property. See PIN (aka Parcel Identification Number).

**Property Profile**   A report formulated by title companies identifying basic statistics of a particular property. Some companies may charge a small fee for this report, but quite often they are free.

**QRP**   A Qualified Retirement Plan, such as a Self-Directed IRA. One in which you can control the investment decisions, including real estate tax lien investments.

**Quiet Title Action**   1. A proceeding to establish the plaintiff's title to land by bringing into court an adverse claimant and thereby compelling him either to establish his claim or be forever after stopped from asserting it. 2. An action filed in civil court to test and/or perfect title to real property. 3. A notice to the world of a pending claim to real property. 4. To request of the court an order to quash any and all subsequent claims.

**Range**   Columns of a mapping grid formed by range lines in six-mile increments. Identified as east or west of the Meridian. Example: R3E = Range Three (columns) East (of the Meridian).

**Real Property**   1. Land and what is generally affixed, erected, or growing upon it. 2. That which is construed as immovable, except crops. Generally a synonym for real estate.

**Recourse Clause**   Legal language in a loan contract that stipulates what a lender can do to collect from a borrower who is in default on a loan.

**Redemption**   Refers to the procedure by which the legal property owner (the title holder) or a vested interested party (such as a tax lien investor) pays the tax collector the amount required to cancel or invalidate the tax lien on the real property.

**Register of Deeds (aka County Recorder)**   A government office where written instruments are recorded for public notice.

**REO (Real Estate Owned)**   Property owned by a bank. Sometimes, you can get the bank to finance the purchase of these properties.

**Reserves**   Amount of liquid assets that a borrower has left after paying all costs of the transaction.

**RESPA (Real Estate Settlement and Procedures Act)**   Federal law that requires lenders to disclose settlement costs (GFE and HUD-1) as well as the procedures for consumer disclosure.

**Review of Assessment**   All real property is evaluated by local government appraisers with the express purpose of determining an assessed value in order to calculate property taxes. Property owners are afforded by law a method of disputing these values that are set for taxation purposes. This phrase describes that process of disputation.

**Rotational Bidding**   A method of auctioning off liens/property. The auctioneer begins with the first parcel listed in the advertisement and asks the party in the first designated seat if they are interested. If not, he proceeds to the party in the second designated seat number, and so forth, until someone accepts. The next lien/property is offered to the party in the following seat until everyone in the room has been offered an opportunity to bid. Then the auctioneer starts all over at the beginning.

**Scavenger Sale**   A term exclusive to large Illinois counties (mainly Cook). A sale that takes place every other year (odd years) for properties previously offered, but not sold at annual tax lien sales. Opening bid on all properties equals $450, and is a premium bid situation.

**Sealed Bid**   A bid made for liens or properties at auction, which are mailed to the administrator of that sale. All bids are open at a set time, date, and place, with the highest bidder being awarded the lien or property.

**Section**   A division of land on a map grid 1 square mile (640 acres) in size. Each township is divided by straight lines and is comprised of 36 sections of land. Sections are then divided into halves and quarters in order to legally describe tracts or parcels of land.

**Self-Directed IRA**   The Individual Retirement Account (IRA) allows annual payments into a tax deferred account. Self-directed accounts allow individual investors to determine how these funds will be invested, as opposed to a trustee or administrator making those decisions.

**Seller Financing**   A process by which the seller of a property agrees to loan the buyer the money to purchase it. See also Land contract and Lease-option agreement.

**Short-Term Capital Gain**   The realized profit on an investment property held for fewer than 12 months.

**Simple Interest**   Interest computed against principal only.

**Struck**   Refers to the action taken by a taxing jurisdiction when transferring title to real property from a property owner to the taxing jurisdiction after a tax sale has taken place and no bids were tendered.

**Subdivide**   To divide a lot, tract, or parcel of land into three or more smaller lots, tracts, or parcels of land for sale or development.

**Subdivision**   A plat of land that has been subdivided.

**Subordinate**   Subject to, or junior to; occupying a lower position, inferior in order.

**Sub-Prime Loan**   A loan that does not adhere to Fannie Mae or Freddie Mac requirements and, as a result, typically charges more in interest and upfront costs.

**Substituted Service**   1. Service of notice of pending action as authorized by statute. 2. To use a publication of notice by newspaper instead of personal service or mail.

**Sub-Taxing**   1. To attach a subsequent year's tax delinquency to a pre-existing lien. 2. To endorse a properly executed Tax Lien Certificate with subsequent tax years, prior to the expiration of redemption.

**Tax Defaulted**   The status of real estate when the property taxes are unpaid and delinquent.

**Tax-Deferred Exchange** A provision of the tax code that allows investors to exchange similar kinds of properties instead of selling those properties and exposing the profits to capital gains taxes. Often referred to as a 1031 in reference to this section of the tax code.

**Tax Extension** 1. The process by which the Tax Collector calculates the tax roll for his/her county. 2. The medium by which the actual tax roll is transferred to printing of the tax bills.

**Tax Lien Certificate** The document issued by a public officer to the successful bidder at a tax lien sale. The prima facie (legally sufficient) evidence of lien position.

**TIL or TILA (Truth In Lending Act)** Federal law that requires lenders to follow certain guidelines for disclosing loan terms, including the APR. Not used on commercial properties.

**Time Value of Money** The concept that a dollar today is worth more than a dollar in the future, because the dollar received today can earn interest up until the time the future dollar is received.

**Title** The owner of record for a parcel of real estate.

**Title Insurance** The insurance policy issued by a title company insuring the accuracy of its search against claims of title defects and against loss and damage resulting from such defects.

**Title Search** 1. An examination of the public record to determine the status of the title of a property (the public record being that of the registry of deeds or recorder's office). 2. To document liens, encumbrances, claims, and defects relating to real property.

**Township** Rows of a mapping grid defining six-mile increments of land by township lines. Identified as north and/or south of the baseline. Example: T6S = Township 6 (rows) South (of the baseline) 36-square-mile tract of land formed by the intersection of Range and Township lines in a map grid.

**VA (Department of Veteran Affairs)** Insures loans made by lenders to eligible veterans.

**Valuation** The estimating of property value for taxation purposes. An appraisal of real property.

**Vested** Having the character or given the rights to absolute ownership; to accrue; fixed; absolute.

**Zero Risk** The virtual risk that a prudent, educated investor has when following the steps and research guidance presented in this book.

**Zoning Codes** A designation of letters and numbers used to divide a city or town into districts in order to regulate the use, and/or structural and architectural design of land and buildings.

# ABOUT THE AUTHOR

Chip Cummings is a recognized expert in the areas of real estate and mortgage lending with over 30 years in the industry and over a billion dollars in real estate volume. He is an experienced investor in both residential and commercial properties, and he bought his first tax lien at the age of 19.

Chip has written hundreds of articles and appeared on radio and television with Fox News, NBC, ABC, and the *Neil Cavuto Show*, and in various publications including *USA Today, Entrepreneur, Wall Street Journal*, and various other newspapers and magazines. He was a featured expert on the cable television series *Sweat Equity*, is the featured financial expert with WXMI Fox 17 TV in Grand Rapids, and also serves as host of a syndicated radio program, *The Financial Fitness Show*, which is heard throughout the country. He is past president of the MMPA and is a licensed mortgage loan originator in Michigan.

As an international speaker, he has addressed groups and organizations of all types, and he is a frequent speaker at conventions and real estate and mortgage events around the country. Chip is a certified continuing education trainer, and has served as an expert witness in state and federal courts. Some of his other books are: *Foreclosure Myths—77 Secrets to Making Money on Distressed Properties,* and *Mortgage Myths—77 Secrets to Saving Thousands on Home Financing,* with Ralph Roberts (both Wiley); *Cashing In on Pre-foreclosures and Short Sales* (Wiley); and *Stop Selling and Start Listening!* (Northwind). Chip also runs a coaching program and investment partnerships for tax sale investments.

To learn more about Chip Cummings, his many success products, or how he can help your organization as a speaker or consultant, visit: www.ChipCummings.com.

To receive a complimentary subscription to his newsletter and *Chip Tips* videos, visit www.ChipTips.com. You can also reach Chip by e-mailing him at info@ChipCummings.com or by calling his office at (616) 977-7900.

Chip lives in Rockford, Michigan, with his wife Lisa and his three children, Katelyn, CJ, and Joe.

# INDEX